CLIMB NOVA SCOTIA

A ROCK-CLIMBING GUIDE

SEAN WILLETT

© Copyright, Sean Willett, 1994

All rights reserved. No part of this book covered by the copyrights hereon may be reproduced or used in any form or by any means—graphic, electronic, or mechanical—without the prior written permission of the publisher. Any request for photocopying, recording, or information storage and retrieval systems of any part of this book shall be directed in writing to the Canadian Reprography Collective, 379 Adelaide Street West, Suite M1, Toronto, Ontario M5V 1S5.

Nimbus Publishing Limited
PO Box 9301, Station A
Halifax, NS B3K 5N5
(902) 455-4286

Design: Kathy Kaulbach, Halifax
Printed and bound in Canada

Canadian Cataloguing in Publication Data

Willett, Sean, 1960-
Climb Nova Scotia
ISBN 1-55109-087-2
1. Rock climbing—Nova Scotia—Guidebook.
2. Nova Scotia—Guidebooks. I. Title.

GV199.44.C3W45 1994   796.5'223'09716
C94-950092-5

Front Cover: Experiencing the exposure of rock-climbing in Nova Scotia: the author on Ludicrous Anachronism, the First Face at Paces Lake, on the Eastern Shore.

CLIMB
NOVA SCOTIA

CONTENTS

PREFACE VII
INTRODUCTION 1

HALIFAX AREA 11
EAGLES NEST 11
- MAIN CRAG 14
- THE BACK SLABS 22
- SCHOOLROOM AREA 23
DALHOUSIE UNIVERSITY 27
POINT PLEASANT PARK 30
BEDFORD HIGHWAY 30

EASTERN SHORE 31
RAILWAY CRAG 32
THE FIRST FACE AT PACES LAKE 34
THE MAIN FACE AT PACES LAKE 46
- NORTH BUTTRESS 50
- SOUTH BUTTRESS 69
- THE DEEP SOUTH END 82
NEVERLAND 86
GIBRALTAR ROCK 90
GIBRALTAR LAKE 90
HOWE LAKE 90
SALMON RIVER LAKE 90
SHIP ROCK 91

SOUTH SHORE 93
CHEBUCTO HEAD 93
TERENCE BAY 93
PEGGYS COVE 95
PADDYS HEAD 96
LIVERPOOL 97

PREFACE

When I was growing up in the foothills of the Wasatch Mountains of Utah, outdoor recreation such as hiking, camping, skiing, and mountain-climbing was well-accepted as a normal part of everyday life. I had early exposure to the various forms of mountaineering through my father, who regularly took me and my brothers and sisters on hiking and climbing trips through the peaks of the Utah Rockies. I particularly remember one early mountain-climbing experience: when I was ten years old, my father and I joined a Wasatch Mountain Club hike to the summit of Little Black Mountain, above Salt Lake City. What should have been an easy hike became an adventure of near-epic proportion when a late spring snowstorm caught us unprepared. We boldly—and naively—continued to the top through near white-out conditions, without parkas, boots, or gloves. I retain a vivid memory of hiking back down the trail with numb hands and toes, wiping my runny nose on the sleeves of my sweatshirt until they hung down to my knees as sodden lumps of snow and half-frozen snot. After that experience, I was hooked: this climbing stuff was fun!

While these trips were really just hikes, the experience of high mountain peaks and the goal-oriented nature of mountain hiking inevitably led to a desire for more interesting challenges. By the time I was fourteen, I found myself tying into the end of a rope and scrambling up the steep limestone crags of Millcreek Canyon, just minutes from my house in Salt Lake City. In an effort to ap-

VIII

pease my overly concerned mother, I took a course in technical rock-climbing, which exposed me for the first time to the soaring granite buttresses of Little Cottonwood Canyon. Although the following decade saw my climbing experiences broaden into ice-climbing and alpine mountaineering, and take me to such destinations as Yosemite Valley, the Canadian Rockies, and the Alps, Little Cottonwood Canyon remained my home climbing area—and clean desert granite my venue of choice.

Thus it was with some apprehension that I packed up in 1988 to Nova Scotia, where the distinct lack of mountains seemed to mark a decline in my climbing days. The next couple of years seemed to support that view, as other demands prevented me from investigating the possibilities of climbing in my new home. It wasn't until the summer of 1990 that I even made inquiries about climbing in the area.

My first climbing experiences in the province were not particularly encouraging. On my first trip to Eagles Nest, I couldn't believe that the crags I found were the entire area and I spent several hours fruitlessly searching for something bigger. Jeff Holmes took me on my first tour of the Paces Lake crags, even though he was also relatively new to the area and was relying largely on secondhand information. We seemed to have a hard time finding any of the routes Jeff had heard about—and it was only later, as I got to know Jeff better, that I realized he could rarely find the routes he had *climbed*, let alone those he hadn't! We wandered around the base of the

First Face, finally starting up a nasty-looking thin crack with no idea if it had ever been climbed or not. I got up about ten metres before making the brilliant observations that the rock was steep, and that two years sitting at a desk was not good training. I backed off, and we found something easier to climb that day.

A year later, I returned to that still-unclimbed thin crack with Dan Price, one of the pioneers of climbing at the lake. Danny was keen to have a go, and smoothly climbed past my previous high point. As the rock steepened, he slowed down, scrabbled for a foothold, then flew off. His first two pieces of protection ripped out, and he was left hanging, with one last piece of protection between him and disaster. After a few more trips with Danny, I realized he always climbed that way—it seemed he spent as much time in the air as on the rock! That thin crack remained unclimbed for two more years and many climbing excursions in the area, until I finally felt bold enough to climb the route that was subsequently named Emotional Vampires.

Accustomed as I was to the desert heat and clean white granite of Little Cottonwood Canyon, I found bushwhacking through dense forests, fog, and swarms of blackflies to reach Nova Scotia's small, lichen-covered crags an entirely different kind of experience. Eventually, my misgivings gave way to an appreciation of the unique opportunities afforded to those with an adventurous spirit and large supply of bug repellent. The setting of the climbing area is exquisite, with its unique combination of eastern forests, lakes, or ocean coastline providing some of the finest scenic locales I have ever seen. Although the season is short, it is worth waiting for the disappearance of snow, winter fogs, spring fogs, and early summer infestations, because the summer and autumn months provide ideal weather for climbing. Those with access to a canoe will find the many of the approaches both shorter and more aesthetic; many of my finest climbing days ended with a quiet paddle across the lake at sunset.

Another new attraction for me in Nova Scotia was the quantity of undeveloped rock. Climbing in Nova Scotia in the 1990s affords possibilities for new route development that haven't existed for decades in more-developed areas such as Utah. Even at Paces Lake, the major area, there remains great potential for new climbs; the rest of the province is largely unexplored as far as climbing is concerned, and numerous undiscovered crags undoubtedly await intrepid explorers. In times of inclement weather or unbearable bug density, exploring for new crags became an alternative to climbing, and my partners and I spent many hours, even days, portaging the canoe up rivers or bushwhacking through the forest in search of climbable rock. Occasionally we even found some. Of course, there were also such experiences as the trip up the Salmon River during which we spent six hours wandering, hopelessly lost, dragging the canoe through dense forest. There wasn't a drop of water in sight—even from the tops of the trees, which we could reach, thanks to our climbing skills.

Ultimately, it was necessary for me to change some of my habits in order to enjoy climbing in Nova Scotia; fortunately, that adaptation came easily and at a time when much of the climbing community was making similar changes. The last decade has seen a shift in climbing style towards short, very difficult free climbs, commonly protected by pre-placed bolts. Such climbs typically require that a climb be prepared in advance by cleaning, bolting, and, often, practising the moves prior to ascent. This sport-climbing style lends itself well to new route development in Nova Scotia, where unclimbed rock is always covered in lichen or moss. I never did develop the skill, or desire, to climb the rock in its natural lichen-covered state or to clean it on lead, so I was quite happy to adopt the new style of cleaning climbs on rappel, whether bolts or natural protection were to be used.

I was fortunate to have done much of my initial climbing in Nova Scotia with Dan Price and Tony Veling, both of whom had climbed for more than a decade in the area and were instrumental in developing climbing routes across the province. Their knowledge and the records of first ascents kept by J.R. (Jayar) Milligan made it easy for me to find my way around the crags, repeat climbs, and, ultimately, develop new climbs. However, verbal exchanges of information are a less than ideal way to attract climbers, as indicated by the small number of people my partners and I have encountered at the more-remote crags. It has always been clear to me that a guidebook would help encourage more activity—and after years of talk, it seems to have become a reality. I hope that this book makes it easier to enjoy trips out to Paces Lake and the other, lesser-known crags, and enables other climbers to take advantage of some of the exceptional experiences that I have known in my years in Nova Scotia.

Publication of this book would not have been possible without the help of numerous people. Special thanks to Jayar Milligan for keeping records of the early climbing history of the area. I owe a personal thanks to Dan Price and Tony Veling for providing me with an introduction to Paces Lake and convincing me that it really was fun to climb lichen-covered rock. Thanks to the following people, who shared their experiences, information and photographs: Brian Adams, Kevin Cody, Chris Dale, Sylvia Fuller, Peter Gilliver, Doug Ives, Mike Moyles, and Heather Reynolds—and any others I may have forgotten. (A brief note on the photographs used in this book: uncredited photos are by the author or from his collection.)

AN OVERVIEW

Mention of the Maritimes is likely to generate images of scenic coastlines, sailboats, lighthouses, and secluded fishing villages: a postcard from Peggys Cove. Although rock-climbing is not normally associated with Canada's east coast, Nova Scotia's rugged relief is not only beautiful, but also provides significant climbable rock to those willing to explore.

The geology of the province is complex, particularly in the north, where the Appalachian Mountains cut across the northern mainland and Cape Breton Island. Historically, most of the climbing in Nova Scotia has been concentrated around the Halifax area, either on the quartzite of the Goldenville formation, which outcrops along the Eastern Shore, or on the granite intrusions of the South and Eastern Shores. The soft, sedimentary rock that characterizes much of the Fundy coast is not suitable for climbing, although some erosion-resistant rocks might be found by a concentrated search. The greatest, but still largely uninvestigated, potential for climbing is in the northern highlands and Cape Breton. The variable geology and high relief of these areas are conducive to good climbing, but the climbing community of Halifax has considered these regions too far away for regular exploration. Certainly, climbing has occurred in Cape Breton—there was even a guide (*Climb Cape Breton*, by John Read) published in the 1970s—but this publication was mostly an auto tour of small crags visible from the road. Because information about climbing in Cape Breton is sketchy, *Climb Nova Scotia* steers away from discussion of Cape Breton and focuses on mainland Nova Scotia.

The quality and quantity of climbing in Nova Scotia cannot compare to the conditions offered in the Rockies or a well-established area like British Columbia's Squamish region, but what the province's climbing experiences

Sean Willett on the first ascent of Fairy Crack, Neverland. Photo: Peter Gilliver

lack in grandeur are more than compensated by their distinctive character. The relative isolation and small number of visitors has allowed most climbing areas to retain a wilderness atmosphere that seems remarkable, given the ease with which they can be reached from the population centres of the province. Climbing in the province has avoided the rapid development and associated crowding problems that are common in other climbing areas across North America. It is still common to be alone on the crags, even on a warm summer afternoon. The major climbing areas all overlook water, and their scenic beauty—whether it is the view over Bedford Basin, Paces Lake, or other bodies of water—makes even long belays a pleasant experience.

WHEN TO COME

The harsh climate of the Maritimes makes for a relatively short climbing season. Spring is a hit-or-miss proposition, as it can be cold, wet, and foggy well into June in Nova Scotia. However, there are usually a few good climbing days between March and June, and depending on the year, there can even be more than a few. With the warm weather of summer comes the onslaught of blackflies, and climbing often stops entirely for two or three weeks in June, resuming when drier conditions herald a welcome decline in the blackfly population. It cannot be stressed strongly enough that blackflies are no joke: at full intensity, their ferocity can make it all but impossible to walk through the woods, let alone climb or belay.

The best climbing in Nova Scotia is midsummer through early fall. Typical temperatures in July and August are perfect for climbing, and unlike most other regions of the eastern continent, Nova Scotia rarely suffers from the high humidity that can make strenuous outdoor activity so unpleasant. Fall comes late to the Maritimes: September is usually a good climbing month, and October and November always provide a few opportune days, although the weather gets increasingly cold and wet as winter approaches.

USING THIS GUIDE

The experienced climber will find this guide straightforward. The basic information needed to select a suitable climb is provided, including location, difficulty, and quality. The climbers and dates of first ascents (FA) have been noted where they are known. Location is described in the form of "topos" (sketches and descriptions) and written descriptions. The Yosemite Decimal System (YDS) has been used to describe difficulty; most North American climbers are familiar with this system.

KEY TO TOPO SYMBOLS Ratings and quality have also been assigned to individual pitches (P.1, P.2, etc.) on multi-pitch climbs.

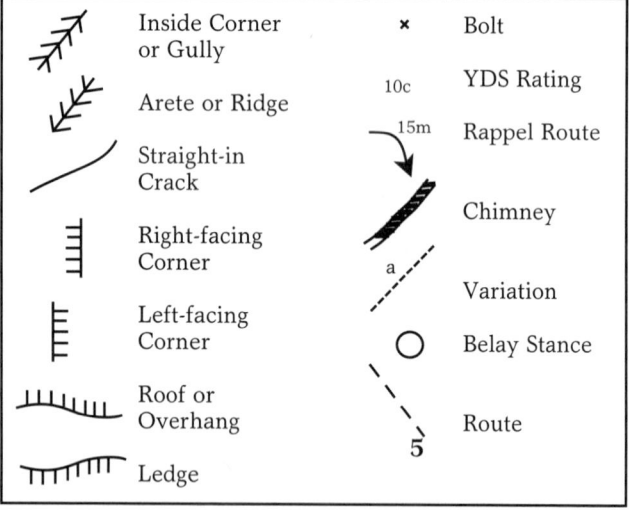

Rating systems can suffer from local calibration, particularly in isolated areas such as Nova Scotia; although every effort has been made to ensure the accuracy of ratings, all these climbs can prove to be relatively easier or harder than those at climbing areas elsewhere. However, ratings in the province do not seem to vary by much from those at other areas visited by Nova Scotia climbers: this has been confirmed by visitors from outside the province, although the suggestion has been made that climbs in Nova Scotia are somewhat harder than climbs of equal grade in Western Canada.

The star system has been adopted to give some indication of the quality of a climb. While this method is clearly subjective, some climbs are notable for their quality rock, situations, or technical demands, while others are characterized by particularly unaesthetic, dirty, or dangerous climbing. Climbs have been assigned values of zero through four stars based on a consensus on their quality. Stars that accompany the variation subsections of some climbs apply to the pitch, including the variation.

Subsections titled "Pro" (short for "Protection"), provided at the end of each route description, deal with the quality and ease of protecting the climb on lead and offer a list of gear that might not otherwise be carried. It is assumed that the leader will be carrying a typical rack, consisting of wired tapers (Rocks or Black Diamond Stoppers in sizes 4 to 10), medium-sized slung or wired chocks (Black Diamond Stoppers, sizes 8 to 12; or Hexentrics, sizes 5 to 9), and a few medium-sized spring-loaded camming devices (SLCDs), such as Wild Country Friends, sizes 1.5 to 3. This rack is just an example: every climber has his or her preferred brands and styles, and

CLIMBING AREAS

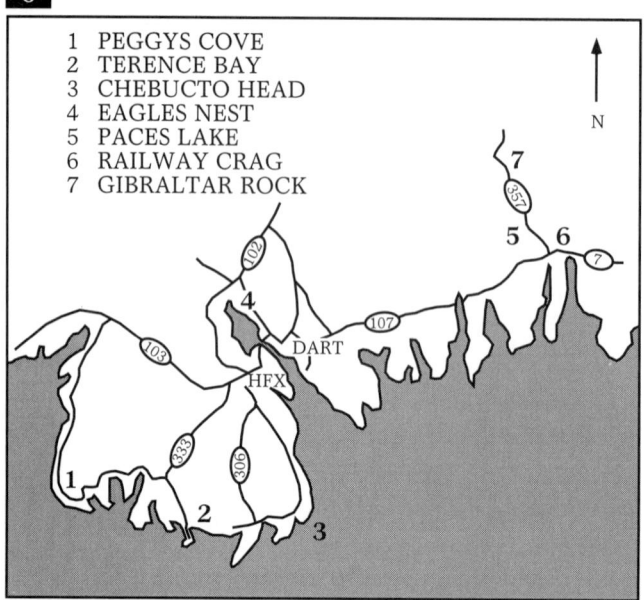

1. PEGGYS COVE
2. TERENCE BAY
3. CHEBUCTO HEAD
4. EAGLES NEST
5. PACES LAKE
6. RAILWAY CRAG
7. GIBRALTAR ROCK

most climbs can be adequately protected with a sufficient variety of gear. Special requirements are generally noted and include thin cracks that need exceptionally small wired chocks, such as Micro-Nuts or RPs, and wide cracks that need large chocks, such as size 10 or 11 Hexentrics or large-size Friends. Occasionally, passive chocks are difficult to place because of flared or overhanging cracks without rest stances. In these cases, SLCDs of a particular size are recommended as useful in the "Pro" section. Small SLCDs refer to Metolius TCU(three-cam units), Wild Country Friends under size 1.5, or equivalents. Medium SLCDs include #1.5 to #3 Friends. Large SLCDs refer to #3.5 Friends or larger. Where bolts or chain anchors are present, they are noted. In Nova Scotia, chains have been placed so that the leader can lower to the ground with a fifty-metre rope.

ACCESS

Access is emerging as a major issue at climbing areas across North America. Even with a relatively small community, climbers in Nova Scotia are not immune to the potential problems. In contrast to western provinces and states, most of Nova Scotia is privately owned, which means that each crag and climbing area has a different property owner with different attitudes and concerns.

The two main areas near Halifax are Eagles Nest and Paces Lake. (Eagles Nest, part of a Bedford city park, is called Eagle Rock by the city planning department; however, most climbers know the area as Eagles Nest. To further complicate matters, the name listed in the Nove Scotia Gazeteer is Eagle Nest!) The city has no official position on climbing in the park, but officials are aware of the climbing activity; the Bedford Recreation Department has even offered rock-climbing clinics at Eagles Nest. On the other hand, the crags at Paces Lake are on private property that has at least three different owners. Most of the Main Face is owned by the family of Mark Hamilton. While Mark is supportive of climbing on the property, he would like to keep track of who is using the area, so permission is required to climb there. Mark has granted permission to all members of the provincial association Climb Nova Scotia to climb on his property, and climbers are encouraged to join that organization if they intend to use the area regularly. For information, contact Climb Nova Scotia through Sport Nova Scotia, P.O. Box 3010, South Halifax, N.S. B3J 3G6.

ENVIRONMENTAL IMPACT

As the number of climbers in the province increases, so will the environmental impact and attendant access problems. Aside from the general concerns of maintaining a clean environment, a few specific points should be addressed.

Trail erosion at the top and base of the cliff is the main environmental problem caused by climbers at the Eagles Nest area. Please be conscious of this, and take care not to aggravate the problem. Nearly all the top-rope anchors at the main crag can be reached by leading an easy (under 5.6) pitch. This saves a trip to the top and avoids additional traffic near the lip of the cliff. Also, avoid the trail from Shore Drive up to the main crag; erosion of this access route needlessly annoys the residents whose yards the trail crosses.

The Paces Lake areas do not attract as much traffic as Eagles Nest, and the impact of climbing activity has been less serious. The largest impact comes from camping. The landowners have always been tolerant of camping, although climbers should get permission to spend the night and be careful to minimize their impact on site. A popular camping area can be found on top of the Main Face, in the hollow between the North and South Buttresses. Use the outhouse at the cabin near the top of the "E" Gully, above the Main Face.

Another potential problem is parking at the boat ramp near the First Face at Paces Lake. In recent years, so many people have been parking there that drivers with boat trailers have been having trouble turning near the ramp. Climbers should not add to the problem.

Try parking at the top of the hill, fifty metres back from the boat ramp.

New route development invariably leads to environmental impact. In the Maritimes, the main impact on the rock is the destruction of vegetation. While climbers can't avoid clearing the rocks of potentially hazardous moss and lichen, they need not cut down larger bushes or trees. If fixed anchors are to be used, please ensure that they blend in with the colour of the natural rock as much as possible. The wet climate, particularly on the sea cliffs, quickly rusts fixed metal anchors, so fixed pitons should be avoided. Bolts don't rust as quickly, but stainless steel bolts last longer and are safer: they are a must on the sea cliffs.

CLIMBING ETHICS

Ethical questions in climbing are typically concerned with issues of style of first ascents, because style determines the character of climbs in an area and because new climbs have a considerable impact on the environment. On subsequent ascents, climbers generally try to respect the original style of a climb. The issue of climbing ethics in Nova Scotia is difficult to address in other than general terms. The climbing community has never been sufficiently large or homogeneous to develop a unique style or ethical creed for the area. Historical information is also lacking; first ascents have not always been recorded, and the style of those ascents has been particularly difficult to recover.

As well, the style of first ascents has been highly variable. Most first ascents were done in traditional "ground up" style, in which climbers start from the bottom, placing all protection as they ascend. But many climbs, particularly at the harder grades, have probably not been "on sight," because of the necessity of cleaning the route of moss, lichen, and other organic hazards so prevalent in the region. Cleaning is often done on rappel, and whoever does the cleaning usually makes the first lead. Rappelling and cleaning a route also makes it convenient to top-rope at least parts of a climb to make sure it will "go," and climbers have taken advantage of this opportunity prior to leading a climb.

Bolts and pitons have been used in the area and have often been placed on rappel during the cleaning process; the emphasis of most climbers in the area has been on safety rather than on maintaining a strong ethical style. However, this tendency has not led to a proliferation of bolts in the area; the majority of routes are protected entirely by natural gear.

Modern sport-climbing, with full bolt-protected ascents, began in Nova Scotia in the 1990s, following trends in the rest of the country that date back to the mid-1980s. Sport climbs are protected mostly or entirely by bolts placed on rappel. First ascents or redpoint (first no-falls) ascents are generally proceeded by "working" a route on top-rope or lead. Sport routes are designated as such in route descriptions, which provide more-detailed descriptions of protection.

As in all climbing areas in North America, a few basic rules should be followed in Nova Scotia. Don't use pitons or place bolts on established routes, and please don't remove any existing pitons or bolts.

As the major population centre, Halifax has also been the centre of the climbing community in Nova Scotia. It is no surprise, therefore, that the areas near Halifax—particularly Eagles Nest—see the most climbing activity. The major universities in Halifax have helped to attract people with more climbing experience from other provinces or countries where climbing is more common. More recently, Dalhousie University has played a more direct role, bringing the first major indoor climbing wall to the Maritimes.

EAGLES NEST

The climbing area at Eagles Nest consists of three small bands of quartzite with no more than fifteen metres of relief. In spite of the limited amount of rock, Eagles Nest remains Nova Scotia's most-popular climbing area. The close proximity to Halifax/Dartmouth is undoubtedly the main reason for the popularity of the area, but there is also something to be said for the quality and variety of climbing available.

The gentle angle, low height, tree anchors, and easy top-roping access make the cliff popular with beginners and introductory classes, but there are also more challenging possibilities for the expert, with several hard sport climbs and good bouldering scattered throughout the area. Eagles Nest is primarily used as a top-roping area, as the quartzite does not easily take natural protection. However, half a dozen climbs have recently been equipped with bolts for protection, and this has encouraged more leading in the area. Several other climbs have good natural protection; these are noted.

The environment leaves something to be desired, with the profusion of litter and broken glass serving as a constant reminder of the price of proximity to the city. Still, the setting can be beautiful, particularly on a warm summer evening, with the sunset over Bedford Bay, and the harbour bridges and lights of Halifax visible across the water.

The history of climbing in the area is a little vague. First-ascent information is sketchy, given the history of the area as a top-roping area. Although all the climbs have been led at some point, no attempt has been made here to systematically document first ascents. Most of the early development at the Back Slabs and Main Crag, including some bold and dangerous leads on natural gear, was done by Tony Veling, Dan Price, and Jayar Milligan. The Schoolroom area was opened, cleaned, and climbed by Sean Willett and Heather Reynolds. The later phase of bolted sport climbs was done by Tony Veling, Sean Willett, Peter Gilliver, and Olivier Maydew.

APPROACH

Eagles Nest climbing area is located in Admiral's Cove Park in the town of Bedford, at the head of the Bedford Basin (see map). To reach the area, take Highway 7 north from Dartmouth. Take the Bedford exit to the left, then the first left at Eaglewood Drive into the residential area surrounding the park. From Halifax, take either the MacKay Bridge to Highway 7 or the Bedford Highway through

EAGLES NEST CLIMBING AREA 13

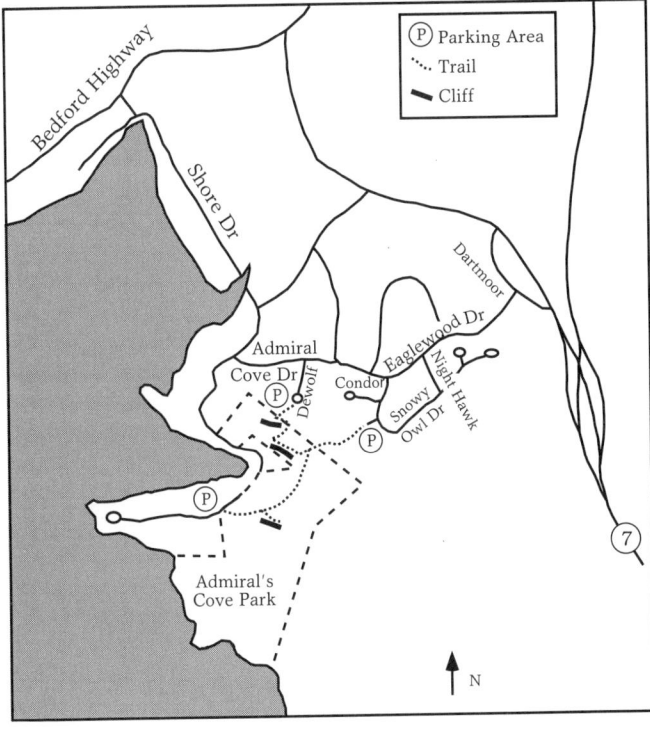

Bedford, turning right under the railroad tracks to reach Shore Drive.

Because the Main Crag can be seen and reached from Shore Drive, this entrance attracts many climbers; however, the resulting trail erosion makes it preferable to choose one of the other park entrances. An entrance off Snowy Owl Drive provides the best parking and shortest approach to the Main Crag; there is also an entrance from Dewolf Circle, directly behind the Back Slabs in the town's residential area. Once in the park, climbers can reach any of the crags described below by using the trail system.

MAIN CRAG

The main cliff in the Eagles Nest area is clearly visible from Lake Shore Drive below. The base of the climbs can be approached from either end of the cliff, although access is slightly easier from the Nursery Slab side (left). It is also common to rappel or down-climb Inconsequential between Sea Gully and the Evening Wall. Top-ropes can be set from the trees along the trail on top, although some of the trees are beginning to show the wear of repeated use. A long sling is useful for sling-shot (bottom) belays. Some of the bolt and chain anchors used for lowering off after leading the sport climbs can be reached from the top for top-roping, but because of the loose gravel and rock at the top of the cliff, scrambling down to the anchors without a belay is not recommended. Chains can be reached safely on rappel or with a belay from above.

ROUTE DESCRIPTIONS

1*   **NURSERY SLAB**   **5.0 TO 5.6**

The low-angle slab with several cracks, located at the left end of the cliff, is a popular area for classes and first climbing experiences. The slab can be climbed virtually anywhere, with variable difficulty. Trees are available for top-rope anchors, although overuse is starting to show. The top can be treacherous, due to loose gravel and the slope.
Pro: Fair to good.

MAIN CRAG

1 NURSERY SLAB
3 THE OVERHANG
8 SEA GULLY
10 EVENING WALL
12 THE CAVE
13 BIG MAC

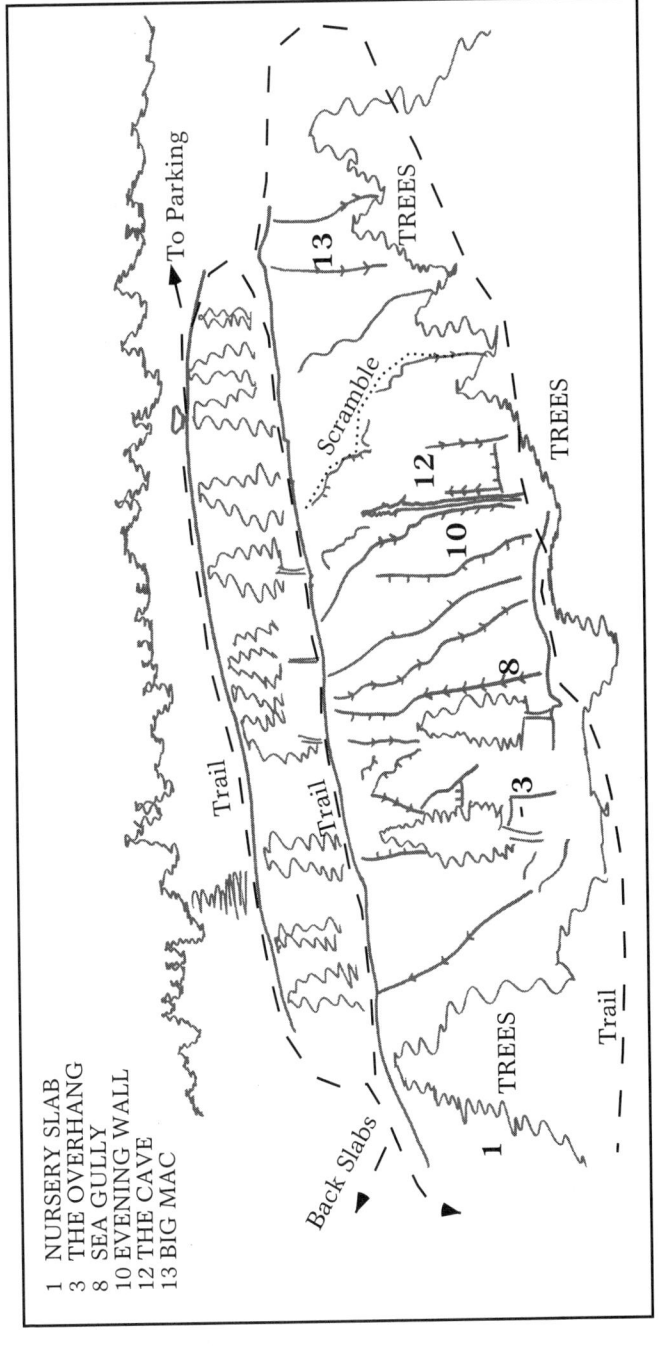

HALIFAX AREA

Note: *The following climbs start from a flat ledge with a large tree.*

2**   BOOMIN' SYSTEM   5.6

Sport Climb

Climb the steep left wall of the dihedral to a ledge. Follow the left edge of the face. If the climbing seems too difficult, just move around the corner to the left, where the going is much easier. Leading this climb is a safe and convenient way to set a top-rope on the Overhang (see description 3). It is best to belay from ledges left of the base of the climb, although someone recently (and thoughtlessly) ripped out the trees that served as a belay anchor.

Pro: Three bolts, chain anchors.

3**   THE OVERHANG   5.8

The forbidding cavelike overhang is climbed out to the left and up the crack to the top. This is a common top-rope problem; it is not unusual to see climbers stuck inside the chimney, unable to move.

Pro: Difficult, but not impossible, to protect on lead.

4**   NO MAN'S LAND   5.10 TO 5.11

Sport Climb

This climb follows the orange overhanging wall to the right of the Overhang and the blocky wall of Kestrel (see description 5), and traditionally stays in the finger crack to the left of the blocky holds. The route is easier if the holds to the right are used. Because No Man's Land lies directly below the eroding gully that serves as top approach for the Overhang, it tends to get dirty after a rain.

Pro: Three bolts, chain anchors up over the edge.

OVERHANG AREA

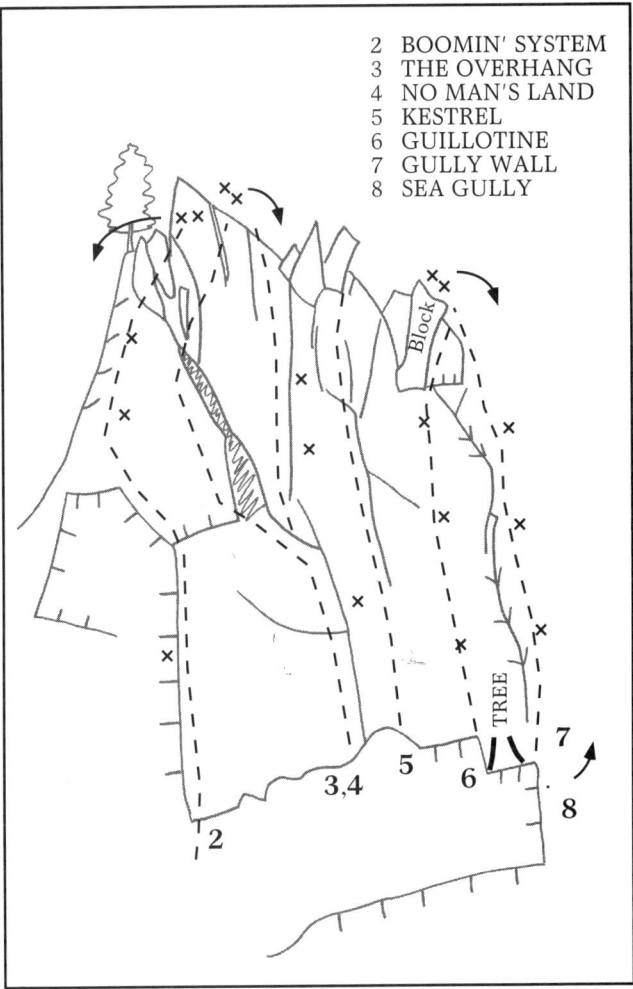

2 BOOMIN' SYSTEM
3 THE OVERHANG
4 NO MAN'S LAND
5 KESTREL
6 GUILLOTINE
7 GULLY WALL
8 SEA GULLY

5*   **KESTREL**   5.9

Extending along a series of flakes and blocks on the right side of the overhanging face, this climb, which includes some loose rock, is poorly protected on lead unless some of the bolts on No Man's Land are used.

6**   GUILLOTINE   5.10a

Sport Climb

A large, dangerous-looking block, perched on the lip of the wall, marks the top of the climb. The best route is to the right of the guillotine block, or traverse under the roof to the right. The block seems to be solid, in spite of its appearance.

Pro: Three bolts, chain anchors.

7**   GULLY WALL   5.6

Sport Climb

Located on the wall to the left of Sea Gully (see description 8), this friction and face climb extends over two small bulges on the wall between the arete and the Sea Gully dihedral. Climbers can also tackle the arete to the left.

Pro: Three bolts, shares chains with Guillotine.

8**   SEA GULLY   5.5

This climb ascends the prominent corner of the gully. Good cracks lead over a small block and up a clean dihedral to the top. A small but sturdy tree at the top makes a good toprope and rappel anchor.

8a*   VARIATION:
BLACK STREAK   5.5 TO 5.7

The wall between Sea Gully and the arete to the right offers some good climbing.

9   INCONSEQUENTIAL   4TH TO 5.2

As its name suggests, this broad, broken slab between the arete to the right of Sea Gully and the Evening Wall (see description 10) can be climbed anywhere without much difficulty.

EVENING WALL CAVE AREA

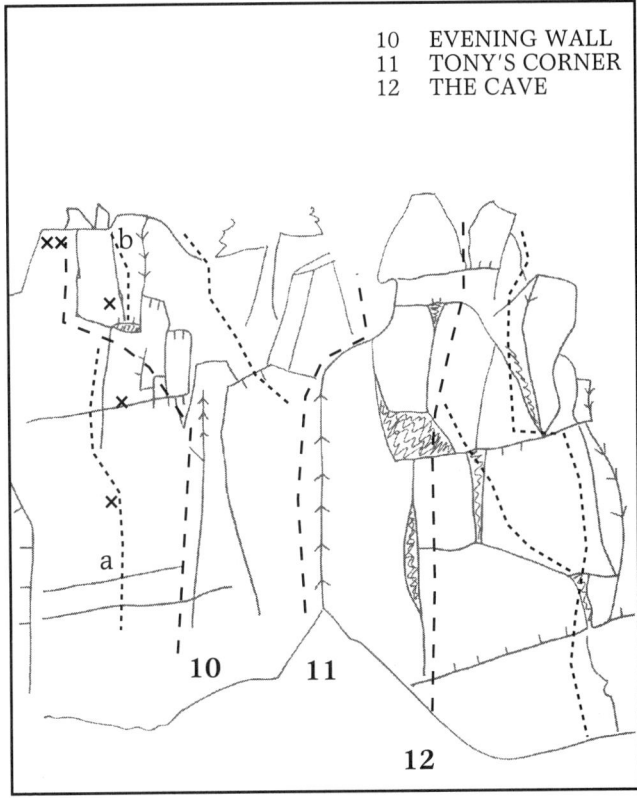

10 EVENING WALL
11 TONY'S CORNER
12 THE CAVE

Note: The Evening Wall and variations, which follow, can be top-roped from the chains at the top of the wall. However, the chains cannot be safely reached from above. It is necessary to rappel or be belayed over the edge from one of the trees higher up.

10***   EVENING WALL   5.9

This is the cleanest, most continuous climb at the Nest. Start in the cracks on the right edge of the face; climb up about six metres, then step left to reach a good crack in the centre of the face. This crack is climbed up the overhanging headwall.

Pro: Can be climbed entirely with mid-sized chocks and SLCDs, or by using the top bolt on the Double Direct (see description 10b). Use chain anchors in either case.

10a***   VARIATION: DIRECT 5.11b/c
Sport Climb

A difficult sport route. Climb the lower face directly, past two bolts, to gain the upper crack. Don't use the cracks to the right of the start, although they are temptingly within reach.

Pro: Three bolts, chain anchors.

Tony Veling on an early lead of the Evening Wall, Eagles Nest (c. 1980). Photo: Dan Price Collection

10b***   VARIATION:
             DOUBLE DIRECT   5.11c

Sport Climb

Climb the Direct, then finish the final headwall by using a thin crack just left of the right edge. Avoid the good crack to the left (the regular route) and the arete to the right. Contrived, but challenging.

Pro: Three bolts, chain anchors.

11   TONY'S CORNER   5.4

This climb ascends the short corner to the right of the Evening Wall.

12**   THE CAVE   5.5 TO 5.7

This wall offers several routes, known collectively as the Cave (named for the niche halfway up the main crack system). A small roof at the base provides an interesting start for most routes. There are good crack routes in the centre and up the right side.

Pro: Good protection is provided by small to medium chocks and SLCDs.

13**   BIG MAC   5.5 TO 5.7

Out of sight from the other routes at the far right side of the cliff is a clean wall with several corners, just short of the talus slope. Many variations are possible. The main route follows a crack-and-corner system to a large tree on a ledge just below the top. Scramble off left from here, or take one of the variations to the right.

Pro: Wires and medium chocks. Big sling for the tree.

13a**   BOLT VARIATION   5.6

Sport Climb

Follow a face line to the right of the protectable cracks.

Pro: Four bolts, big sling for the tree. Clip the first bolt from the ledge to the right.

13b*   VARIATION: WANTON DESTRUCTION   5.9

Traverse the ledge to the right of the big tree at three-quarter height. This short route climbs small flakes and cracks directly behind the twenty-metre spruce tree leaning against the cliff.

Pro: Small wires, RPs. (If you panic, grab the tree behind you!)

THE BACK SLABS

The Back Slabs, primarily a top-roping area, are located about fifty metres up the hill and back (north) into the forest from the main cliff. The area is accessible from a trail that starts at the top of the Nursery Slab, or can be reached from a short trail leading off Dewolf Circle. A fire destroyed the forest behind the crag in the spring of 1993, but stopped just short of the top-roping trees at the cliff's edge.

ROUTE DESCRIPTIONS

1*   FLYING DUTCHMAN   5.8 TO 5.10+

This climb extends directly over the one-metre roof at the left end of the back slabs. Climb the smooth slab up under the roof,

then surmount the roof by whatever means possible. The right side is easier; the left is quite difficult. The name commemorates Tony Veling's many attempts (ultimately successful) to lead the climb.
Pro: Possible, but potential groundfall.

| 2 | FOXHOLE | 5.8 |

This is a series of thin cracks and face holds on the smooth slab six metres right of Flying Dutchman.
Pro: Top-rope problem.

| 3 | SLIDING BOARD | 5.5 TO 5.8 |

The short slab at the far right can be climbed with or without one or both of the two thin cracks.
Pro: Top-rope problem.

SCHOOLROOM AREA

The Schoolroom area is several hundred metres from the Main Crag in the direction of Halifax and is best approached by a trail that starts from Shore Drive, about two hundred metres up the hill from the curve below the main crag. This small crag was cleaned and developed in the early 1990s and has a number of short easy-to-moderate routes, characterized by large positive holds. This is a good area for beginners and classes; most of its routes have good lead protection with a standard rack of chocks.

SCHOOLROOM AREA

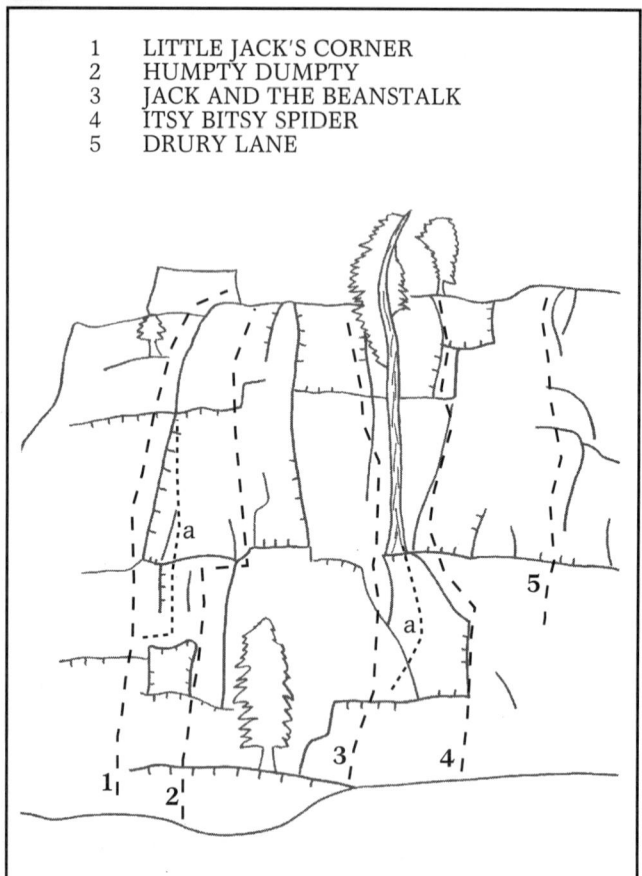

1. LITTLE JACK'S CORNER
2. HUMPTY DUMPTY
3. JACK AND THE BEANSTALK
4. ITSY BITSY SPIDER
5. DRURY LANE

ROUTE DESCRIPTIONS

1 **LITTLE JACK'S CORNER** 5.5

Climb the left side, facing the dihedral on the left of the roof.

1a VARIATION 5.6

From the top of the detached block one-third of the way up, climb the steep wall on the

right of the arete and continue to the right of the corner.
Pro: Fair to good.

2* HUMPTY DUMPTY 5.6

Reach the roof by climbing over from the top of a detached block to the left, or climb directly up the slabs below. Climb directly over the roof. Finishes by the large boulder on top. Several variations are possible. There is one bolt and a good crack in the boulder to use for a top anchor.
Pro: Fair to good.

3 JACK AND THE BEANSTALK 5.4

Start in the dihedral, climbing up to and around either side of the big tree. Continue directly up the crack line. Use a two-bolt anchor at the top.
Pro: Good.

3a VARIATION 5.5

Climb the cracks on the wall directly below the tree. A nicer climb than the regular route.
Pro: Good.

4 ITSY BITSY SPIDER 5.4 TO 5.5

Start in the steep corner below and to the right of the big tree. Stay to the right of the tree, follow the crack upwards, and finish the climb above a small bulge with a right-facing dihedral, just below a small tree on the lip of the cliff. Use a two-bolt anchor at the top.
Pro: Good.

5   DRURY LANE   5.4 TO 5.5

Take the slab and crack line at the right side of the cliff. There is some loose rock on this climb.

Pro: Fair to good.

BOULDERING

Good bouldering awaits throughout the Eagles Nest area, particularly in the vicinity of the Back Slabs. There are several challenging problems on the wall at the far right end of the slabs, around the corner from Sliding Board. The trail between the Back Slabs and the Nursery Slab passes just above several large boulders, the largest of which has a perfect hand crack (5.8) splitting its main face. This boulder is large enough—and the landing bad enough—to warrant a top-rope for the crack or several other problems to either side. Another problem follows the arete to the right of the hand crack.

Just to the left of the split boulder is a smaller boulder with a protruding nose of an overhang. A series of awkward mantle problems surmount this overhang; they are generally easier to the left and harder to the right. It is also possible to completely traverse the lip of this boulder.

There is also plenty of bouldering on the upper steps of the main crag where the Snowy Owl Drive trail first reaches the cliff. Although the rocks are covered with graffiti, and sometimes broken glass, the area is worth exploring: there are several good thin cracks and other problems.

More bouldering is found throughout

the woods around the Schoolroom area; the prominent boulder at the top of the Schoolroom cliff poses a few challenging problems.

DALHOUSIE UNIVERSITY

Opportunities for climbing in Nova Scotia were greatly expanded with the installation of an indoor climbing wall at Dalhousie University in 1992. Although not large by modern competitive and sport-climbing standards, the wall is challenging and fun, and provides welcome relief from the long Maritime winters. The climbing wall, nearly six metres high and ten metres wide, is constructed from textured panels equipped with movable modular holds. There are two overhanging relief structures. Unroped bouldering is allowed on the lower three metres of the wall; belay anchors (but not ropes) are available for the upper wall.

The existence of the Dalplex wall owes much to a donation made by Brian and Hetty Adams on behalf of their son Ben, who died in 1991 at the age of fourteen, as the result of a congenital heart problem. Although he had started climbing only a year before—by saving money from his paper route for classes and equipment—he quickly became an avid, and active, climber. After learning the basics, he became a regular at Tuesday evening climbs out at Eagles Nest (although he had to miss out on the post-climbing sessions at the Granite Brewery). Ben's enthusiasm for climbing motivated his parents to leave a memorial to their son that they felt certain would please

The first climbing competition at the Dalplex Climbing wall, 1993. Photo: Brian Adams

---

him, and climbers who visit Dalplex will find the plaque in memory of Ben on the right side of the wall.

To use the wall at Dalplex, a climber must be accredited. This involves completing

a short safety check with one of the instructors, covering harnesses, knots, and belaying—a ten-minute process that costs about $15. The accreditation is entered in the Dalplex computer so that on subsequent visits staff can check the climber's status. Accreditation is for life, and accredited climbers can use the wall any time the fieldhouse is open, unless the wall is reserved for classes. Climbers may either use their own rope, harnesses, slings, and belay devices, or rent these at the equipment desk.

Contact Dalplex about scheduling an appointment for accreditation or enrolling in climbing classes—one of which, an all-day course, includes accreditation for future use of the wall.

POINT PLEASANT PARK

For the truly desperate, there is some bouldering (buildering, to be precise) to be found on the old forts in Point Pleasant Park. The Martello Tower can be very challenging, depending on the state of mortar upkeep. A long brick wall near the water between the anchor and war memorial also offers some interesting problems.

BEDFORD HIGHWAY

Several roadcuts along the Bedford Highway near Halifax offer some short ice-climbs in winter—nothing higher than about eight metres, but enough for some good ice-bouldering. The roadcuts are near the Halifax end of the Bedford Highway, just short of the Joseph Howe turn-off.

EASTERN SHORE

The best climbing in Nova Scotia is found on the Eastern Shore, near the Halifax-Dartmouth metro area. Two cliffs overlooking Paces Lake, as well as several smaller crags scattered throughout the Musquodoboit Valley, have served as the principal playground for Nova Scotia climbers since the late 1970s. With up to eighty metres of relief, the Main Face at Paces Lake is the largest vertical piece of granite yet developed by climbers in Nova Scotia.

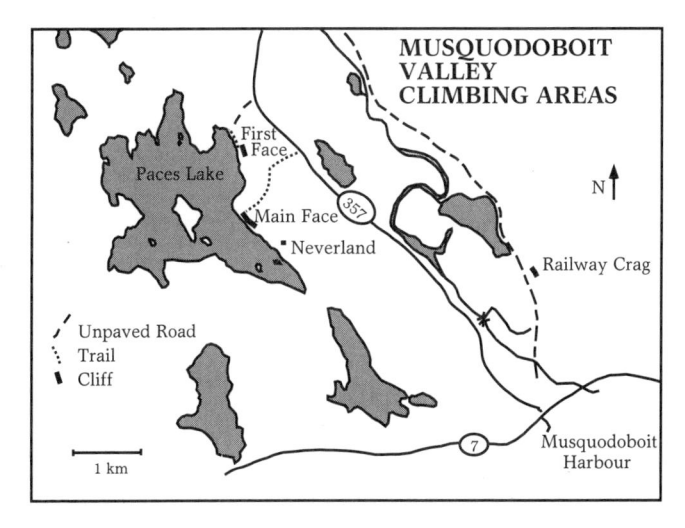

MUSQUODOBOIT VALLEY CLIMBING AREAS

- First Face
- Paces Lake
- Main Face (357)
- Neverland
- Railway Crag
- Musquodoboit Harbour (7)

- Unpaved Road
- Trail
- Cliff

1 km

N ↑

The Musquodoboit Valley extends west from the town of Musquodoboit Harbour, forty-five kilometres northeast of Halifax and Dartmouth on Highway 107. At the Musquodoboit Harbour junction—marked by the railway museum and RCMP station—turn left onto Route 357, which follows the Musquodoboit River towards Route 224. (See the accompanying map and the "Approach" section within each area description for more-detailed information.)

RAILWAY CRAG

This small crag is visible from the main highway across the river, but is not visited often. The cliff offers some good, relatively clean rock and a decent height—about thirty metres. There is also excellent bouldering in the valley behind the cliff, although access, through the debris of a large fire-burn, is a problem.

APPROACH

Cross the Musquodoboit River at the bridge one kilometre west on Highway 357 from Musquodoboit Harbour. Follow the road to its end at a gravel pit near a small lake. From

RAILWAY CRAG

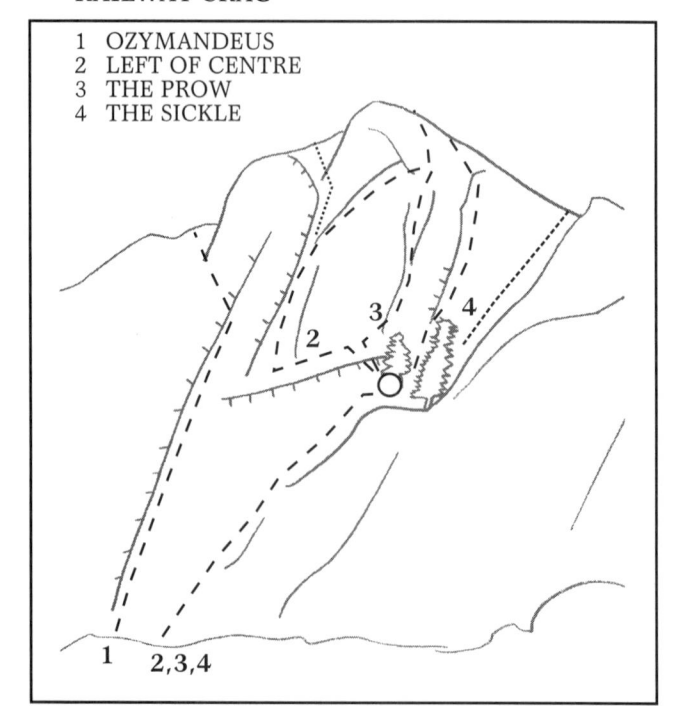

1 OZYMANDEUS
2 LEFT OF CENTRE
3 THE PROW
4 THE SICKLE

there, hike along the abandoned railway line or follow the small trail just above the railway line. In either case, a ten-minute walk leads to the cliff.

ROUTE DESCRIPTIONS

1 OZYMANDEUS 5.6

Follow the corner system up the left side of the cliff.
Pro: Good.

Note: The next three routes share the first pitch, which follows a ramp through the overhanging lower wall to a major sloping ledge that crosses the face (5.6).

2* LEFT OF CENTRE 5.7
   FA: Unknown

From the left side of the sloping ledge, climb a right-facing corner, then follow an arching flake line across the main face to finish up the central prow.
Pro: Excellent.

3* THE PROW 5.10
   FA: Top-rope only

This climb extends directly up cracks and shallow dihedrals in the centre of the wall.
Pro: Should be leadable, but protection is sketchy at the bottom.

4 THE SICKLE 5.11-5.12 ?**
   FA: None

The arching crack directly above the belay in the trees has resisted all attempts thus far, in spite of perfect protection. This may have something do with the overhanging angle and difficult, off-hand dimensions of the crack.

THE FIRST FACE AT PACES LAKE

The First Face at Paces Lake provides some of the cleanest, steepest routes in the region. Handy access and hard rock have made this face popular with "after-work" evening climbers. The rock is more sharply fractured and angular than typical granite in the region and provides some excellent thin-crack and face climbs. Recently, the steep faces between the main crack lines have proven receptive to bolt-protected sport climbing, and the First Face currently provides the highest concentration of hard sport climbs in the province. The most prominent features on this cliff are the centrally located "7"-shaped dihedral and roof of Pyramid and the large arching roofs on the right side.

Top-roping is possible with either top belays or very long slings. The trees at the top are set back from the cliff top, making a long sling or second rope necessary for bottom belays. Existing chain anchors are set below the rim so that they may be used to top-rope from the base with a fifty-metre rope.

APPROACH

To reach the First Face, follow the unpaved private road that turns to the left, 6.1 kilometres from the Musquodoboit junction. The 1-kilometre road leads in to a boat ramp on the lake. The face is visible from the end of the boat dock. If it is a busy day, park at the top of the hill, above the boat ramp. From the boat ramp and dock, a trail leads south along the lakeshore for about 200 metres, to a large talus slope just below the cliff. Climb the talus to the base of the cliff. A trail follows the base of the cliff and provides access to the top, up a scrambling route in a short corner on the right side.

Sean Willett works out on the face of Ludicrous Anachronism, First Face at Paces Lake.

FIRST FACE AT PACES LAKE

1. ANNIVERSARY WALTZES
2. SCRAPE AND PILLAGE
3. INDIAN SUMMER
4. PYRAMID
5. SINS AND TRANSGRESSIONS
6. SNAKESKIN
7. EMOTIONAL VAMPIRES
8. APRIL COOL
9. LUIDRICROUS ANACHRONISM
10. SLAVE TO FASHION
11. MEA CULPA
12. A PUFF OF BLUE SMOKE
13. BLACK DIAMOND

EASTERN SHORE

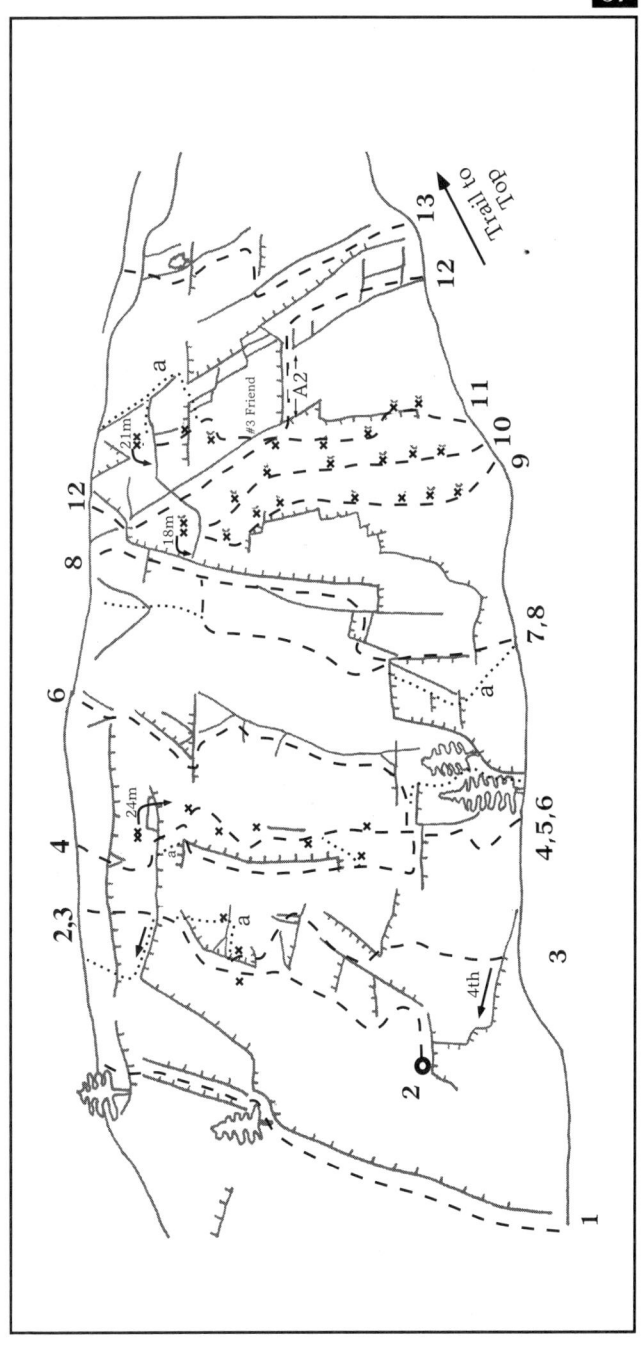

ROUTE DESCRIPTIONS

1*   **ANNIVERSARY WALTZES**   5.6
FA: Chris Dale
September 1978

Climb the blocky ramp past a pine tree at the base of two steep, shallow dihedrals. Climb the rightmost dihedral, although it may be easier to move to the left near the top.
Pro: Standard rack.

2**   **SCRAPE AND PILLAGE**   5.9
FA: Sean Willett and Heather Reynolds
August 20, 1991

Scramble up to a ledge about ten metres to the left and above the start of Pyramid (see description 4). Traverse right from the belay three metres along a small ledge, to start in a dirty corner with a scruffy tree. Traverse left out of the corner, then up and right following a series of corners and faces, keeping to the left side of four successive roofs. The ramp above the bolt is committing. Climb the final three-metre step directly, or traverse left and scramble off. Beware of swinging into some loose blocks in the lower roofs.
Pro: Standard rack. There is a bolt to the left of the last roof and a piton at the top of the ramp.

3**   **INDIAN SUMMER   5.9**
              FA: Sean Willett and
              Heather Reynolds
              November 29, 1992

Ascend the fractured wall directly below the roofs of Scrape and Pillage to a ledge below a right-leaning dihedral. Climb out onto the face to the right, avoiding the large loose block under the overhang. Follow a crack and then the face up and right to a small blocky corner leading to the sloping ledge below the crux ramp of Scrape and Pillage, then continue up the ledge to the top.

Pro: Standard rack. Sparse on the lower face. Some horizontal crack placements.

3a**   VARIATION   5.11
                                   Sport Project

At the bolt above the sloping ledge, traverse right under a small roof to a second bolt. Continue straight up to join Scrape and Pillage above the ramp.

Pro: Two bolts plus the gear for Indian Summer and the top of Scrape and Pillage.

4****   **PYRAMID   5.10d**
                  FA: Dan Price and Tony Veling
                  June 27, 1982

This is a superb climb—clean, hard, exposed, and well-protected. The route is very obvious, with a left-facing dihedral ending beneath a prominent roof. Start to the right of the base of the dihedral, climbing either a poorly protected five-metre wall (5.9) to a ledge, or the tree-filled corner to the right of the standard start. Move left and climb the shattered crack-

and-face past a bolt (5.10b) to gain another ledge at the base of the corner. Lieback or jam the awkward corner until it eases back onto a ramp below the roof. Exit the roof, traverse right about two metres, and climb the overhanging face to a large ledge (5.10d). One last move off the ledge leads to easier ground and the top of the climb. It is also possible to lower off the chains for Sins and Trangressions (see description 5).

This climb was first accomplished in traditional "yo-yo" style—after many attempts—and represents a fine effort by Dan and Tony. The route wasn't repeated for nearly ten years.

Pro: Standard rack, one bolt.

4a****   VARIATION:
           STRAIGHT UP   5.10b
           FA: Tony Veling and Dan Price
           July 1990

From the outside corner of the roof, climb straight up (5.10b) to gain the ledge. The discovery of this variation was made somewhat to the chagrin of the first ascenders, who spent many hours attempting the original finish. This alternative provides a much easier and more direct finish to the climb, and has become the standard route.

Note: The section of the First Face between the Pyramid dihedral and the April Cool corner is steeper than it appears, and provides excellent climbing. There are currently only three routes, but room for more with the thin cracks and seams that abound on this section of the wall.

5**** SINS AND TRANSGRESSIONS 5.11d
FA: Sean Willett
June 1991 (variation 5b)
September 1992 (complete route)
Sport Climb

Continuous difficulty and varied face-climbing make this route enjoyable and challenging. Start as for Pyramid. At the first ledge continue straight up to a bolt. A reach-dependent move leads to a series of small ledges and another bolt at the base of a short thin crack. Climb the thin crack, then move left into the shallow corner below the overhanging wall and follow this corner up and right, then left again to climb the original finish of Pyramid to the ledge and chains.

The first of a new generation of sport climbs in the area, this route represents an increase in dependence on rappel-placed bolts (hence the suggestive name) as well as being a step up in technical difficulty.

Pro: Five bolts and chains.

5a**** VARIATION 5.11d

Start as for Pyramid. At the bolt on Pyramid, traverse right to rejoin Sins below the second bolt. This variation avoids the reach-dependent move at the first bolt on the regular route. A few wired nuts protect the moves up to the bolt on Pyramid.

5b*** VARIATION 5.11c

At the last bolt, traverse right to join Snakeskin (see description 6) and continue up to belay in the trees. This climb is somewhat easier than the regular route. Some nuts are needed for the upper section, which does not reach the usual chains.

6****   SNAKESKIN   5.10a
            FA: Tony Veling and Ted Johnston
            July 1989

An elegant and well-protected climb. Start as for Pyramid. At the first ledge, climb to the right over a disconcertingly loose block to gain a thin crack. Follow this crack up and right to a horizontal crack. Move right at this crack (5.10a), then left, up the face to a small ledge under the roof. Traverse left around the roof and climb the ramp and chimney to the top.
Pro: Standard rack with extra wires.

**7*   EMOTIONAL
            VAMPIRES   5.10c**
            FA: Sean Willett and Sylvia Fuller
            September 29, 1993

This climb follows a thin crack above the large block on April Cool. An awkward mantle leads to the thin crack, which continues to a small roof. From the roof, traverse right to rejoin April Cool or continue straight up through the mossy roof to a ledge and the top.
Pro: Marginal. RPs or Micro-Nuts required. Small TCUs also useful or necessary. A serious lead.

8*   APRIL COOL   5.8
            FA: Kevin Cody and Peter White
            April 17, 1981

This route ascends the prominent corner in the centre of the face. Climb a short wall and

series of broken ledges to the top of a large block below and to the left of the corner. Stem or face-climb (harder) up into the corner, and continue up to a ramp leading to the top.
Pro: Excellent. Mid-sized cracks.

8a*   VARIATION   5.8
             FA: Dan Price
             1990
Climb the diagonal crack in the large block.

Note: The face between the April Cool corner and the big arch of Puff of Blue Smoke (see description 12) is highly fractured and textured, providing excellent face-climbing of an unusual nature for granite. The fine positive holds combined with the steep angle (vertical to overhanging) make for challenging sport climbing, and the wall currently provides three excellent bolted sport routes. Various combinations of the routes are also possible.

9*   LUDICROUS
             ANACHRONISM   5.11c/d**
             FA: Sean Willett
             October 1992

Sport Climb

Follow a line up the steep face to the right of the loose corner, which should not be climbed. At the overhanging upper section, an exciting move to the left and upward gains a large hold just above the roof. Shares chains, but not bolts, with Slave to Fashion (see description 10).
Pro: Seven bolts and chains.

10***   **SLAVE TO FASHION**   **5.11b/c**
FA: Sean Willett
October 1992   *Sport Climb*

Take the line to the right on the steep, fractured face. The wall starts steeply, but eases back in the middle section above the fourth bolt. At the small roof, follow a left-arching flake to the last face-moves on the overhanging upper section. Some loose rock to the left of the middle section should be avoided.
Pro: Six bolts and chains.

11****   **MEA CULPA**   **5.12a**
FA: Sean Willett
September 1991   *Sport Climb*

This difficult climb on the elegant face below the big roofs offers unusually fine face-climbing on inset holds. Climb the shallow dihedral and arete below the first roof, exiting onto the face to the left above the second bolt. Cross the diagonal crack above the first roof and traverse right, then upward, to reach the second roof. Climb directly through the upper roof, using the left-leaning crack (5.12a).
Pro: Seven bolts, #3 Friend for the diagonal crack, chains. There may also be a fixed nut above the last bolt. Note that the first bolt can be clipped from the large talus block to the right.

11a***   VARIATION   5.11b
An awkward move to the right (5.9) exits the roof onto a ledge, avoiding the last crux.
Pro: Additional medium-sized nuts for the upper crack to the top, or traverse back left to the chains.

11b*   VARIATION   5.11b

Join Puff of Blue Smoke (see description 12) at the diagonal crack, following the crack to the left of the roof (5.7).

Pro: Five bolts, one #3 Friend, several small to medium nuts.

12   **A PUFF OF**
          BLUE SMOKE   5.7, a2
          FA: Kevin Cody and Tony Veling
          October 23, 1982

Start at the large left-leaning arch on the right side of the face. Free-climb through large loose blocks up to the metre-wide roof. Aid left under the roof, exiting left into the diagonal crack, which is followed to the top (5.7).

Pro: Thin pitons needed.

13***   **BLACK DIAMOND**   5.9
          FA: Unknown
          June 1990

This climb ascends the left-leaning diagonal crack to the right of the prominent arch and overhang. Traverse right on a narrow ledge to a second crack about ten metres up. Follow this crack to a small tree; move right again at the tree.

Local climbers cleaned this route, but before they could return to make the first ascent, chalk marks mysteriously appeared up the entire climb. The explanation? Two visiting climbers and former employees of Black Diamond Equipment had been in the area and unknowingly made the first ascent.

Pro: Excellent.

THE MAIN FACE AT PACES LAKE

The longest climbs in the region are found on the Main Face at Paces Lake, which offers routes up to three pitches in length—although most are only one pitch, and the longer climbs are broken up by the major ledge systems that cross the face. Because the face rises directly out of the lake, it is difficult to view, and climbers must cope with an unusual procedure: approaching routes from the top. The Main Face—despite the name—is not a single face at all, but consists of a domed northern buttress and a broad, more broken southern buttress. The longest routes are on the North Buttress, but the steepest routes tend to be on the flanking wall overlooking the gully north of the face, or on the steep central section of the South Buttress.

APPROACHES

The best way to reach the Main Face is by canoe from the road and boat ramp at Innis Cove (see First Face Approach, page 34). A ten-minute paddle gets you to the face, with the added advantage of being able to see prospective climbs. For the more pedestrian visitor, a private trail leads in directly overland from the highway, starting on a curve on Highway 357, 4.8 kilometres northwest of Musquodoboit Harbour. The best parking is on the left (southwest) side of the road. The trail is difficult to spot from the road, but it is marked with flagging tape, and once established, is easy to follow. A twenty-minute walk leads to a cottage overlooking the lake;

NORTH BUTTRESS

SOUTH BUTTRESS

50'

MAIN FACE AT PACES LAKE

EASTERN SHORE

47

the climbing area extends from this cottage south. The trail continues along the top of the cliff for its entire length and eventually leads down the far side to the lake, providing easy access to many of the climbs. Climbers frequently set up top-ropes from the trail above the North Buttress. Otherwise, to reach the base of the climbs it is necessary to use one of the approaches described below; most of these are marked with flagging tape.

Climbers in the "E" Gully area of the North Buttress. Photo: Doug Ives

The "E" Gully

The "E" Gully climbs on the North Buttress (whose names all start with the letter *E*) are approached from the gully that cuts down to the right (facing the cliff) on the north side of the Main Face. Access to the top of the gully is by a series of trails leading down from near the cottage. Several steep dihedrals rise directly out of the gully to the top of the face. Ecstasy, one of the first climbs documented at Paces Lake, ascends the largest of these dihedrals. Dry access to climbs farther right on the North Buttress is blocked by the Priceless slab, which rises directly out of the lake at the base of the gully. The sheltered cove at the base of the gully is a good spot for a swim on hot days.

Meatgrinder Rappel

Climbs on the lower section of the North Buttress and the entire South Buttress of the face are best approached by a twenty-metre rappel just to the right of Meatgrinder, the first large corner on the left side of the South Buttress. The alternative is a long scramble over the South Buttress and down the right side of the face. To reach the rappel point, follow an indistinct trail that descends from the highest point atop the North Buttress. One rappel from the tree at the top of Meatgrinder deposits the climber on the trail at the base of the wall.

High Ledge

Several of the pitches on the upper North Buttress are continuations of climbs that start at the base of the face and so are approached from the Meatgrinder rappel or the "E" Gully. However, many of these climbs are continuous only by tradition. Once on High Ledge, at the base of the upper buttress, it is possible to traverse freely—and take any of the other climbs to reach the top. High Ledge is also directly accessible from both ends, near the top of either Ecstasy or Meatgrinder.

South Buttress Trail
Although most routes on the South Buttress are most easily reached from the Meatgrinder rappel, access to the base of these climbs is also possible by using the trail that leads over the top of the face and back down to the lake.

NORTH BUTTRESS
ROUTE DESCRIPTIONS

1**   **ENCHANTMENT**   **5.8**
         FA: Tony Veling and Kevin Cody
         June 14, 1987

Start at the first large corner in the "E" Gully, just to the right of the cavelike overhang near the ground. Climb up the corner until the crack closes off, then take the flake on the right wall to the top. An exposed, exciting finish.

Pro: Standard rack.

2***   **ENERVATOR**   **5.12b**
         FA: Sean Willett
         September 1991   *Sport Climb*

This sport route follows the overhanging arete to the right of Enchantment. Start as for Euthanasia (see description 3). Above the second

bolt traverse left, underclinging a small roof for three metres to the arete. Climb directly over the roof and up the arete for a few desperate moves (5.12b) to the last bolt—and, finally, to the chains.
Pro: Five bolts, chains.

2a**   VARIATION   5.9
The arete can be finished on gear. From the chains, follow a flake and crack up and to the right, finishing at the top of Euthanasia.
Pro: Small to mid-size nuts.

2b***   VARIATION   5.9
Start on Enchantment, but climb right to the arete just below the fifth bolt, above the crux of Enervator. Once past the chains, finish on either Enchantment or Enervator (Variation 2a).

3*   EUTHANASIA   5.11a
            FA: Sean Willett and Dan Price
            July 6, 1991

This route climbs the obvious fist and off-width crack in the centre of the overhanging wall left of Ecstasy (see description 4). Start, as for Enervator, on the small ledge at the base of two small dihedrals leading up to the left side of the large ledge. Stem up the left dihedral past two bolts (5.11a), then step right to reach a flake in the right dihedral that is climbed to the ledge. You'll notice an old bolt on this ledge near the base of the crack. Climb the strenuous, overhanging jamcrack to a second ledge. Continue up the crack through the final five-metre overhanging headwall (5.10) to slabs at the top. The rope tends to jam in the top crack.

Pro: Three bolts, medium to big gear, up to ten centimetres.

3a**   VARIATION   5.10

The crack can be joined from Ecstasy at the first ledge, thereby avoiding the 5.11 dihedral and making this entirely a crack climb.

North Buttress, Main Face, Paces Lake: The "E" Gully rises from the lake at the lower left corner.

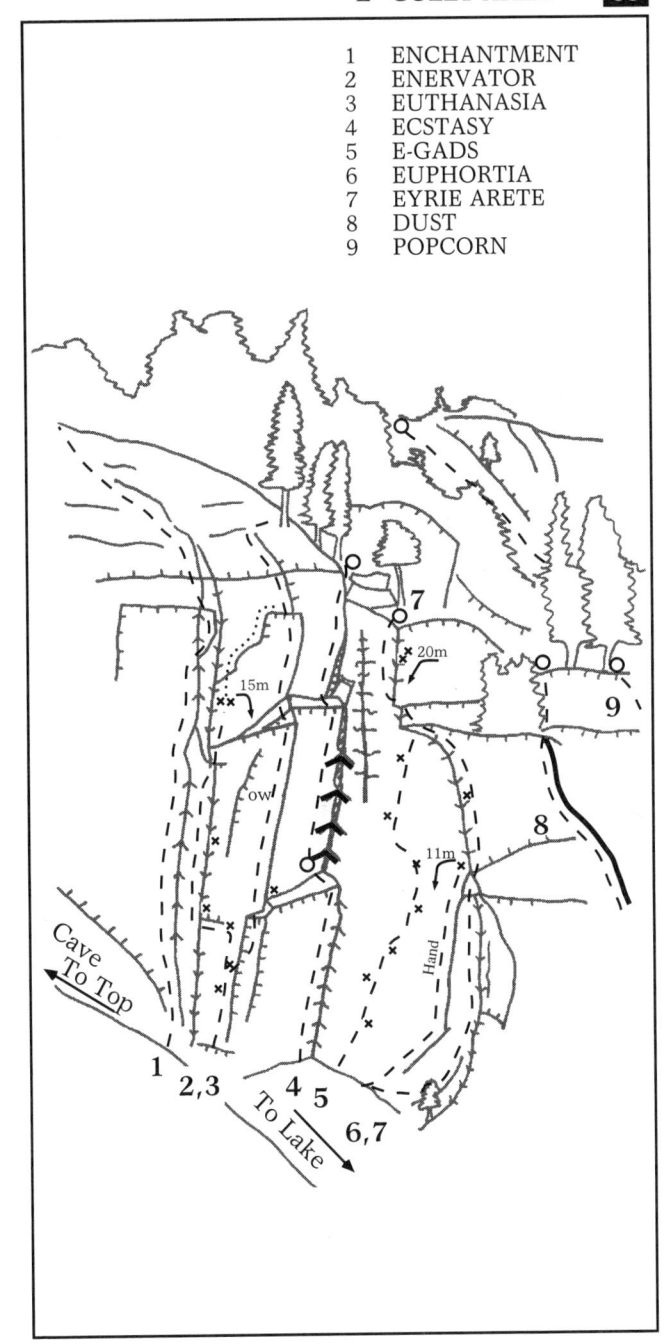

NORTH BUTTRESS "E" GULLY AREA

53

1 ENCHANTMENT
2 ENERVATOR
3 EUTHANASIA
4 ECSTASY
5 E-GADS
6 EUPHORTIA
7 EYRIE ARETE
8 DUST
9 POPCORN

EASTERN SHORE

4   ECSTASY   P.1**   5.8
P.2**   5.6

FA: Chris Dale et al.
August 26, 1978

An area classic up an obvious line, this route is frequently wet, but is usually still climbable. Start at the bottom of the large corner halfway down 'E' Gully. Climb the steep corner to a large belay ledge, using the face to the right and the good lieback and jamcrack. The second pitch continues up the blocky chimney to the top. Can be top-roped from the tree at the top.

Pro: Standard rack.

5***   E-GADS   5.12

FA: (Project)   *Sport Climb*

Climbers used to begin the ascent at the centre of the featureless 75° wall to the right of Ecstasy by making their way up the birch tree at the base of the wall. But the tree collapsed and now leans at 45° into the gully, so it is now possible to start climbing directly from the ground. Climbs small edges and crystals for eighteen metres to the top. Start left, traverse right just below half height (almost to the Euphoria crack), then traverse five metres back to the left below the top of the wall.

Pro: Top-rope only. Belay chains, but the climb may not yet be bolted.

6*   EUPHORIA   5.7

FA: Kevin Cody and Peter White
July 26, 1981

Start this climb six metres to the right of Ecstasy near the edge of the face, just to the

right of the birch tree leaning into the gully.
Climb the face over a small spruce growing
out of the wall into a crack-and flake-system,
which is followed to a bolt above a block on
the corner. Rappel off the bolt and block, or
continue up Euphoria Arete (see description 6a).
Pro: Standard rack. May need a rappel sling
to leave on the block.

6a**		VARIATION:
		EUPHORIA ARETE 5.10b
		FA: Dan Price and Sean Willett
		July 6, 1991

From the bolt at the top of Euphoria, step
right around the corner onto the rough face.
Continue up the arete via delicate crystal-
climbing past another bolt to a belay ledge
and a scramble off to the right.
Pro: As for Euphoria, plus two bolts.

7***		**EYRIE ARETE**		**5.10b**
		FA: Sean Willett and
		Heather Reynolds
		August 17, 1991

This airy, exposed arete climb starts as for
Euphoria. At the small spruce, traverse right
below the flake to the edge of the face. Climb
directly up the arete past a large bird's nest to
the bolt at the top of Euphoria. Continue up
Euphoria Arete to a last steep step; climb the
step directly up the corner (5.10b), and finish
at the top of Ecstasy.
Pro: Standard rack, wires, three bolts.

8   DUST   5.6

FA: Chris Dale et al.
August 27, 1978

This climb, which follows the overgrown crack system immediately to the left of the North Buttress, could be a good one if it were clean. Scramble up until it is possible to belay by a tree below the first steep corner, then follow a series of good cracks and corners to the upper buttress ledge.

Pro: Good. Medium to large nuts.

9   POPCORN   P.1****   5.6
                   P.2 *   5.5
                   P.3 **   5.3-5.5

FA: Chris Dale et al.
August 26, 1978

This is a classic, well-protected, and enjoyable climb. The base is reached by traversing a small mossy ledge out of the gully to the right. Follow the break, which starts at the lower left edge of the North Buttress and angles up and right across the face. Climb the break until it is possible to climb over a small bulge onto a ledge. Friction up the slab above to a large belay ledge and tree. The second pitch traverses left along the ledge for five metres, then climbs the slab to a belay on High Ledge. The third pitch climbs the upper slab directly to the top.

Pro: Excellent with standard rack.

LOWER NORTH BUTTRESS

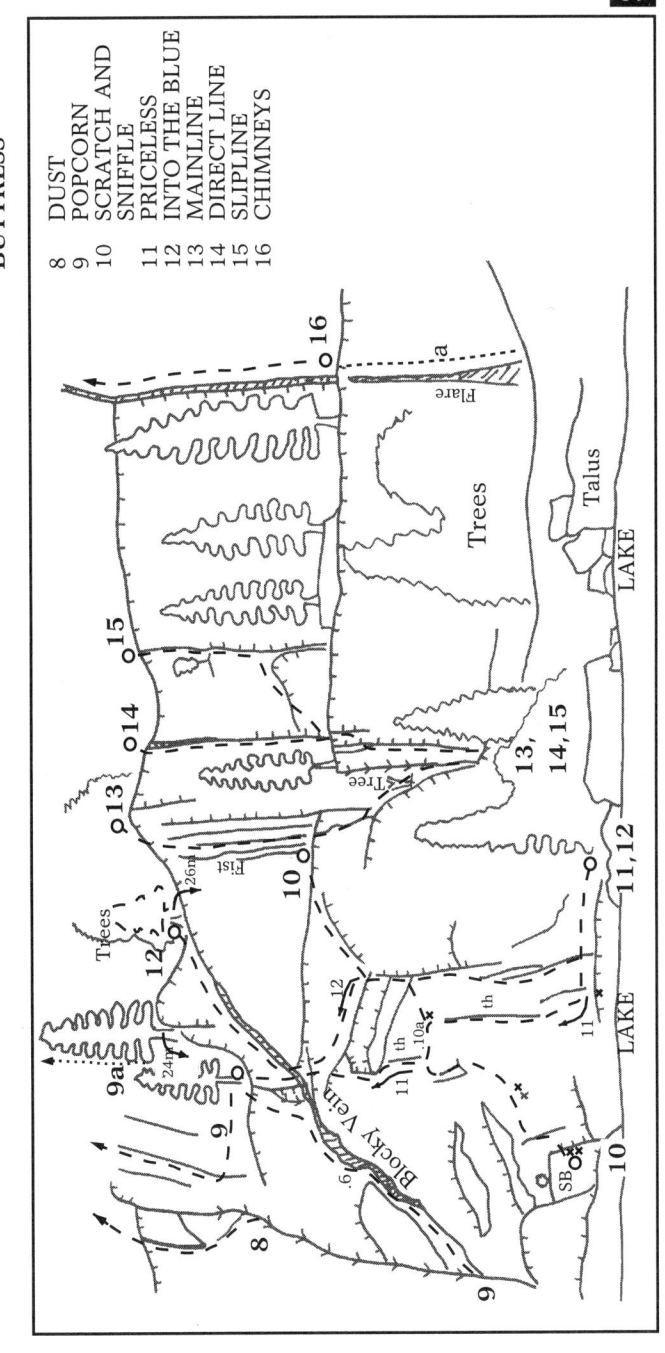

8. DUST
9. POPCORN
10. SCRATCH AND SNIFFLE
11. PRICELESS
12. INTO THE BLUE
13. MAINLINE
14. DIRECT LINE
15. SLIPLINE
16. CHIMNEYS

EASTERN SHORE

9a**   VARIATION: GIMME CRACK CORN   5.6
FA: Jayar Milligan, Dave MacLeod, and Tony Veling
August 1982

Provides a more direct line and nicer climbing than the original second pitch of Popcorn. From the first belay, continue straight up the crack immediately adjacent to the tree to High Ledge.
Pro: Excellent.

10*   SCRATCH AND SNIFFLE   5.9**
FA: Kevin Cody and Mike Moyles
November 1984

Start at the water's edge, on the left side of the slab at the base of the central buttress. Traverse in from the left to a two-bolt hanging belay a few metres above the water. Climb five metres up a left-leaning crack, then exit right past a bolt onto the face (5.9). Step right, then up the crack to join Priceless (see description 11) left of the traverse. Reverse this traverse to the Priceless bolt. Continue right into the corner, which is climbed to the top of the slab, then right to gain the ledge at the base of the second pitch of Mainline.
Pro: Small to medium chocks, two bolts.

10a**   VARIATION   5.10a

Instead of reversing the traverse, continue up the upper section of Priceless. It is possible to rappel twenty-five metres from the belay tree to reach the ledges to the left of the start of Scratch and Sniffle.
Pro: Small wires needed.

Sean Willett and Heather Reynolds practise delicate slab-climbing on Scratch and Sniffle, Main Face, Paces Lake. Photo: Doug Ives

Contemplating a fall in the lake on Priceless. Photo: Jeff Holmes

Note: *Climbs south of, and including, Priceless must be approached from the south, either by the Meatgrinder rappel or the South Buttress trail.*

> 11**** **PRICELESS** 5.10a
> FA: Tony Veling and Jayar Milligan
> November 18, 1982
> FFA: Dan Price, 1983

Danny Price missed out on the first ascent (hence the name), but got the first free ascent. This excellent climb starts at the lower right corner of the large slab that rises directly out of the lake. Step left onto the slab, following a thin seam and crack directly up to a bolt. Traverse left on delicate friction and crystal smears across the slab to the base of a fine finger crack, which ends at an overhanging headwall (5.10a). Swing left around the overhang to gain a series of ledges and a belay at the tree on Popcorn. Continue up Popcorn or rappel twenty-five metres from a tree eight metres to the right of the Popcorn belay to reach the base of Priceless.

Pro: Well-protected once into the thin crack, but protection placed high to the right of the start will prevent a dunk in the lake from low down. RPs or other small nuts useful.

12	INTO		
	THE BLUE	P.1**	5.7
		P.2	5.5
		P.3	5.6

FA: Kevin Cody and Tony Veling
July 25, 1982

Start on the right side of the Priceless slab by climbing the easy crack on the edge of the slab into the small corner; then climb the corner and traverse five metres left, along the ledge. Step right, ascend a short, steep section of broken block, and angle up, slightly leftward, to a belay at a large tree five metres to the right of the Popcorn belay tree. (This first pitch can be scary, because of the exposure over the Priceless slab.) On the second pitch, climb cracks and vegetated slabs to High Ledge. The third pitch extends over a small bulge (5.7) into the corner just left of the overhanging wall and follows this corner to the top.

Pro: Well-protected with standard rack.

13   **MAINLINE** P.1*   5.8
              P.2   5.6
              P.3** 5.7

FA: Chris Dale et al.
September 2, 1978

A long climb up the centre of the buttress begins with lower pitches that are usually dirty, but the last pitch is justifiably popular and is frequently climbed or top-roped on its own. Follow the steep line of cracks at the right side of the central face, starting at the bottom of the corner leading up to the cracked wall; easy climbing for twenty metres leads to a belay tree below the cracks. Directly behind the stance, climb the steep cracks (5.8) into the obvious break and up to a belay among the trees. Scramble up the slabs to High Ledge. The upper buttress is climbed to the right of two parallel jamcracks reaching the top just left of the high point of the buttress.
Pro: Well-protected with standard rack. SLCDs useful for first and third pitches.

14**   **DIRECT LINE**   5.8

FA: Chris Dale et al.
September 1978

To ascend this vertical crack line just right of the first pitch of Mainline, start by climbing the blocky, overhanging dihedral (5.8) to the right of Mainline, continuing to a large ledge. Proceed up the obvious crack, dihedral, and squeeze chimney to join Mainline at the first belay ledge.
Pro: Excellent.

14a*   VARIATION   5.7

Traverse in from the right on the ledge above the crux dihedral. This is the same ledge used to approach Chimneys (see description 16).

15   **SLIPLINE P.1**   5.8
              P.2   5.5
              P.3 *   5.10 a

   FA: Dan Price and Sean Willett
   July 1990.

This route follows the next crack line to the right of Direct Line. Start as for Direct Line, in the blocky dihedral, or traverse in from the base of Chimneys. From the top of the dihedral, move right and climb a crack and flake over the steep step to a belay (5.8). A short, scrambling pitch reaches High Ledge, at the far right of which are several incipient cracks next to a large tree. Climb this face (5.10a) up the five-metre wall, then continue straight up the easy corner or move left to join one of the other climbs.

Pro: Good. Last pitch is essentially a boulder problem off the big ledge. No protection until the hard climbing is over.

16**   **CHIMNEYS**   5.5
   FA: Chris Dale et al.
   September 1978

One of the few moderate routes at the lake, this route, a popular first line for new climbers, follows the obvious deep chimney-and-crack system on the far right of the North Buttress. Scramble in from the right on a large, bushy ledge to gain the base of the main chimney. Stem up the chimney-and-crack system; a large chockstone near the top of the chimney can be passed on the inside or outside. Walk off to the right, to the top of the Meatgrinder rappel station. This route can be top-roped from High Ledge.

Pro: Excellent with standard rack.

16a   VARIATION   5.6

Rather than traversing in from the side, climb the mossy slot below the start of the main chimney. This was the original line.

Note: The remaining climbs on the North Buttress are short one-pitch climbs that start from High Ledge (see Approaches, p.49.) Descriptions of the top pitches of climbs that start lower down are repeated here.

9   **POPCORN P.3****   5.3 -5.5

Climb the slabs on the left side of the upper North Buttress; many variations are possible.

Pro: Poor. Not much on the upper slabs—but not much is needed.

12   **INTO THE BLUE P.3 5.6**

Climb a small bulge into the corner just left of the overhanging wall and follow this corner to the top.

Pro: Good.

17   **ENGAGEMENT**   5.10c

FA: Rick Prenger
1988

This route follows the leftmost of a pair of thin cracks in the overhanging wall, which presents painful and often bloody jams. The crack ends above the overhang (5.10c), but

the climb continues up the slab past a bolt, directly to the top.
Pro: Good in the thin crack—if you can place it and still find a jam. One bolt.

18   ATTACK OF THE KILLER HUMMINGBIRD   5.9
FA: Rick Prenger, Mike Moyles
1988

Take the right-hand thin crack in the overhanging wall, joining Engagement or Into the Blue.
Pro: Good.

19   BLIND MAN'S BLUFF   5.7
FA: Tony Veling and Dan Price
July 1981

Climb the dirty corner to the right of the overhanging wall that has two thin cracks. Continue up the higher crack to the base of a bulge with twin cracks, then follow the right-hand one to the top.
Pro: Good.

19a   VARIATION   5.8
The face to the right of the initial corner can be climbed directly.

20*   DRY IDEA   5.8
FA: Mike Moyles and Tony Veling

Ascend the seam and face on the outside corner to the right of Blind Man's Bluff. Continue up the slab to a crack that is followed to the top.
Pro: Standard rack with some small wires. The slab is a bit run-out.

UPPER NORTH BUTTRESS

- 9 POPCORN
- 12 INTO THE BLUE
- 17 ENGAGEMENT
- 18 ATTACK OF THE KILLER HUMMINGBIRD
- 19 BLIND MAN'S BLUFF
- 20 DRY IDEA
- 13 MAINLINE
- 21 MEN AT WORK
- 22 BIRTHDAY
- 23 UP OVER
- DOWN UNDER
- 15 SLIPLINE

The upper North Buttress of the Main Face at Paces Lake. High Ledge cuts across the bottom of the photo.

CLIMB NOVA SCOTIA

EASTERN SHORE

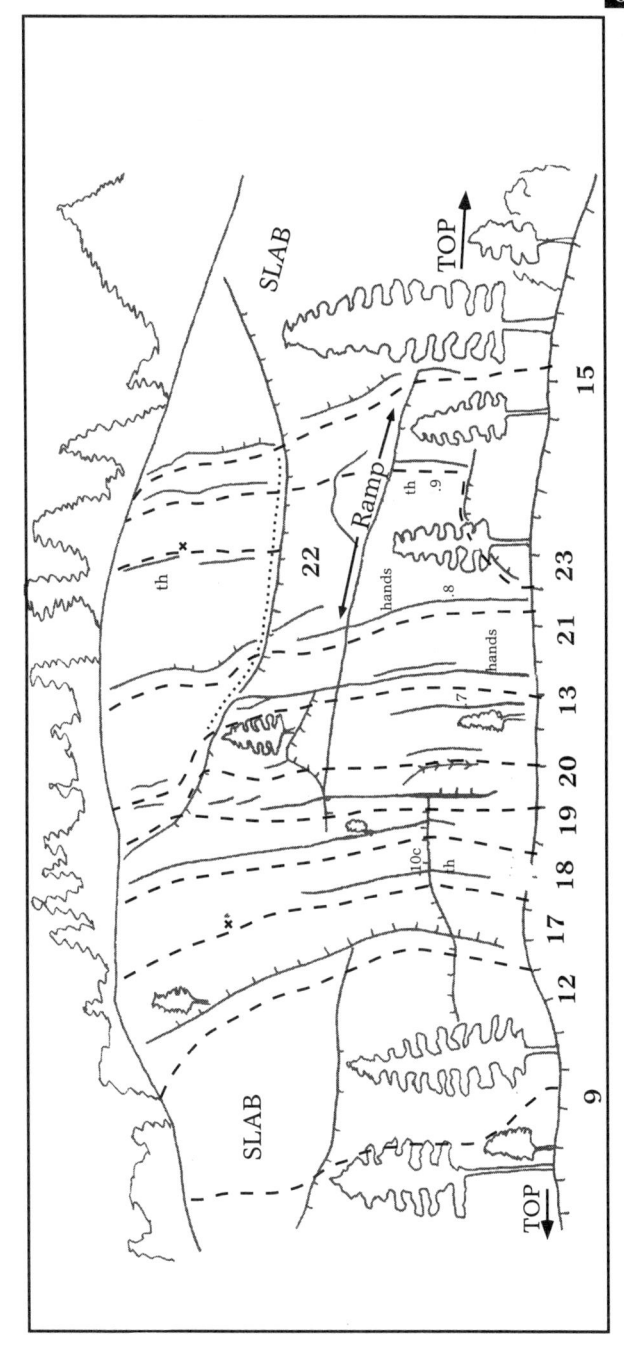

Note: *The third pitch of Mainline (5.7) ascends the rightward of two parallel jamcracks that reach the top just left of the high point of the buttress. See description 13 for details.*

21* MEN AT WORK 5.8
FA: Tony Veling and Dan Price
June 1982

Start up the crack just right of Mainline, follow it over a small bulge, and friction out over the top. Take a hint and try liebacking, which is about a grade easier than jamming.
Pro: Poor at the start, gets better. SLCDs useful.

22** BIRTHDAY 5.10b
FA: Rick Prenger
1988

This climb lies directly below the top of the buttress. Climb Men at Work, Up Over Down Under (see description 23), or Slipline (see description 15) to the ramp below the smooth bulge of the top of the buttress. Climb a seam and the face on the right, past a bolt, over the bulge, into a thin crack, and up to the top.
Pro: RPs or small wires needed. One bolt. Poor protection below the bolt.

23** UP OVER DOWN UNDER 5.9
FA: Glen Donahue and Tony Veling
August 1987

Start just right of Men At Work: hand-traverse right and up on a flake to a vertical thin crack that is climbed through a bulge (5.9), then move right to cracks leading to the top.
Pro: Excellent with standard rack.

Note: The third pitch of Slipline (5.10a) ascends the incipient crack in front of the pine tree at the far right of High Ledge. See description 15 for details.

SOUTH BUTTRESS
ROUTE DESCRIPTIONS

1**   **OSKAR**   **5.9**
FA: Tony Veling and Kevin Cody
August 2, 1987

This route follows the fine finger crack on the south-facing wall to the left of Meatgrinder. Climb directly up the crack, then follow the ramp along the top of the wall to end at the ledge near the rappel tree.
Pro: Well-protected by small wires.

2*   **MEATGRINDER**   **5.8**
FA: Chris Dale et al.
September 3, 1978

Climb the first obvious corner on the left side of the South Buttress. Start with a scramble up the ramp that starts below and to the right of the corner, then climb the short corner into the crack itself. Awkward jamming through a bulge (5.8) leads to a rest in a small niche. Move left from the niche into the groove, which leads to the top.
Pro: Large chocks needed for offwidths.

2a*   VARIATION: DIRECT   5.8
FA: Kevin Cody and Tony Veling
August 1987

From the niche near the top, step right to a thin crack and up.

3***   **NO PURCHASE**   **5.10c**
FA: Tony Veling, Glen Donahue
August 1987

Start to the right of Meatgrinder in a shallow, left-facing dihedral at the top of a long, sloping ramp. The start is tricky and may not be very well protected. Climb up the face and thin cracks for six metres, then cross into a second dihedral to the right. Follow this dihedral and crack straight up through a bulge to end on the ledge to the right of the Meatgrinder rappel.

Pro: Standard rack. Small SLCDs useful for lower crack.

4   **HURRICANE P.1** ** 5.5**
                  P.2 ** 5.9
                  P.3 * 5.8
FA: Chris Dale et al.
September 3, 1978

This often-wet route climbs the largest corner in the centre of the South Buttress. Ascend fifteen metres up the easy crack and corner to a semi-hanging belay below the steep section of the corner. Climb the overhanging corner (5.9) for eight metres, at which point the angle relents, but the rock tends to get mossy. Continue up to a belay on the ledge below a steep crack splitting a final bulge. Climb this crack to the top. This last pitch can be

SOUTH BUTTRESS
HURRICANE AREA

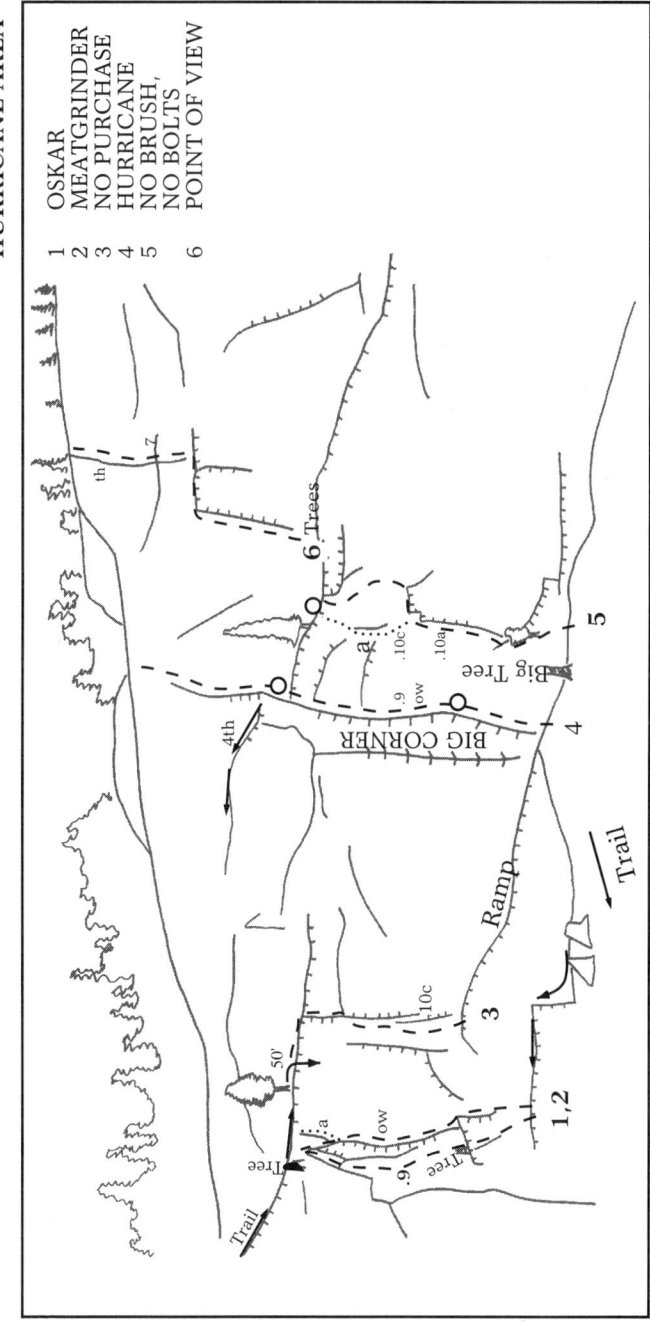

1 OSKAR
2 MEATGRINDER
3 NO PURCHASE
4 HURRICANE
5 NO BRUSH,
6 POINT OF VIEW

EASTERN SHORE

avoided by scrambling off to the left.
Pro: Large chocks needed.

5**   **NO BRUSH,**
                 NO BOLTS   **5.10a**
                 FA: Sean Willett
                 and Heather Reynolds
                 October 11, 1991

The first ascent was done on sight—no previewing or cleaning. Start just right of the big tree right of the Hurricane corner. Climb a ramp into a short, steep dihedral, which is climbed (5.10a) to a small ledge. Traverse five metres right, to the end of the ledge on top of a blocky pillar. Face-climb up to a large roof and traverse left, to end on the ledge at the base of Point of View.
Pro: RPs or small wires are needed to protect the dihedral.

5a*   VARIATION   5.10c
                 FA: Sean Willett
                 and Heather Reynolds
                 October 25, 1992

From the top of the short, steep dihedral, climb the face up and left (5.10c) to a flake-and-crack system. Continue directly up to the ledge.
Pro: Fair. RPs or small wires needed, small to medium SLCDs useful.

6***   **POINT OF VIEW**   **5.7**
                 FA: Tony Veling and Kevin Cody
                 June 1987

This is an airy and fun climb high on the face. Climb No Brush, No Bolts or traverse in from the second belay ledge of Hurricane. Climb a

blocky corner to a ledge below the upper face, then continue over a small bulge into a thin crack, which is followed directly to the top.
Pro: Standard rack. The upper thin crack is very well protected by wired chocks.

6a*   VARIATION   5.6
         FA: Heather Reynolds
         1993

From the top of the big corner, continue straight up to the second ledge, then traverse right to regain the original line. This variation bypasses the crux moves.

Tony Veling seeks aid during an early attempt on Aids.

SOUTH BUTTRESS
AIDS AREA

```
7   SEIZE THE DAY
8   AIDS
9   JEKYLL AND HYDE
```

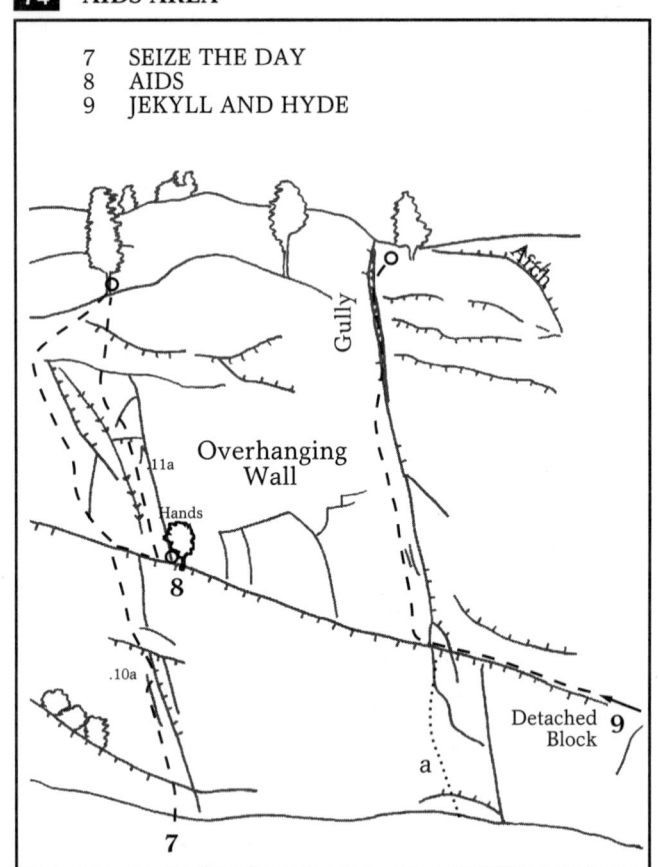

7 **SEIZE THE DAY** **P.1* 5.10a**
                         P.2 * 5.9

FA: Tony Veling and Ted Johnston 1989

In the centre of the South Buttress, about half way up, is a distinctive overhanging wall, smooth and streaked with green. Seize the Day starts directly below this wall. Climb a left-leaning crack to a small overhang five metres up. Swing right through the awkward overhang (5.10a) to gain a crack system, which is followed to a large belay ledge directly below the green wall. Step left around the overhanging headwall and climb a crack and steep corner to the top.

Pro: Fair. Small to medium SLCDs useful for the crux crack and overhang.

8***   **AIDS**   **5.11a**
FA: Tony Veling, Sean Willett, Dan Price, and Jeff Holmes. July 1990. First redpoint some years later.

This is a classic Paces Lake overhanging jamcrack. The first few ascents involved various amounts of hanging and pulling on gear, although it was eventually redpointed. Follows the crack on the left side of the green wall above Seize the Day. Climb the first pitch of Seize the Day or rappel from the top to the belay ledge. The wall above this point overhangs about 30° and is split by an obvious, left-leaning jamcrack. Climb this crack on good—but strenuous—hand and fist jams for about eight metres, until a small horn (5.11a) is gained and the wall eases back. Follow cracks and a short slab to the top.

Pro: Excellent. Medium to large SLCDs.

9*   **DR. JEKYLL AND MR. HYDE**   **5.8**
FA: Tony Veling and Dan Price June 1982

This climb follows the major break to the right of the Aids wall. Scramble along the ledge that cuts into the break from the right. Step left and up into a left-facing corner. Follow this corner-and-flake system to a ledge and belay at the base of a gully. Continue up the gully to the top.

Pro: Well-protected by standard rack.

9a   VARIATION:
        DIRECT START   5.9

Ascend the thin, overhanging face to a sloping mantle on the first ledge, starting just left of a steep, left-facing corner.

Pro: Limited. Small to medium SLCDs.

10***   **MR. PUFF**   **5.7**
        FA: Dan Price and Kevin Cody
        1981

This steep but moderate climb, on the left side of the red, mottled face, starts from the top of a large detached block, which has sheared from the base of the cliff. Reach across from the top of the block and pull up into the right-facing corner, or traverse up from the right. Face-climb and stem up the shallow dihedral and thin cracks. Scramble off left or join Conan (see description 13) to the right.

Pro: RPs or small wires useful.

11**   **DON'T LET GO**   **5.10c**
        FA: Tony Veling, Kevin Cody,
        and Rick Prenger
        June 1987

A steep, challenging climb, long and continuous. Start just left of the arete bordering the mossy gully of Conan, ascending a strenuous overhang right off the ground into the left-leaning grooves. Follow the lower groove until it is possible to climb over a bulge into the

SOUTH BUTTRESS
CONAN AREA

9. JEKYLL AND HYDE
10. MR. PUFF
11. DON'T LET GO
12. THE ABYSS
13. CONAN
14. RAGNAR
15. WEDGE
16. LUNCHBUCKET
17. SLEEPER
18. THE LOST HURRAH
19. SHIVER ME TIMBERS
20. TRIAL RUN
21. PIECE OF CAKE

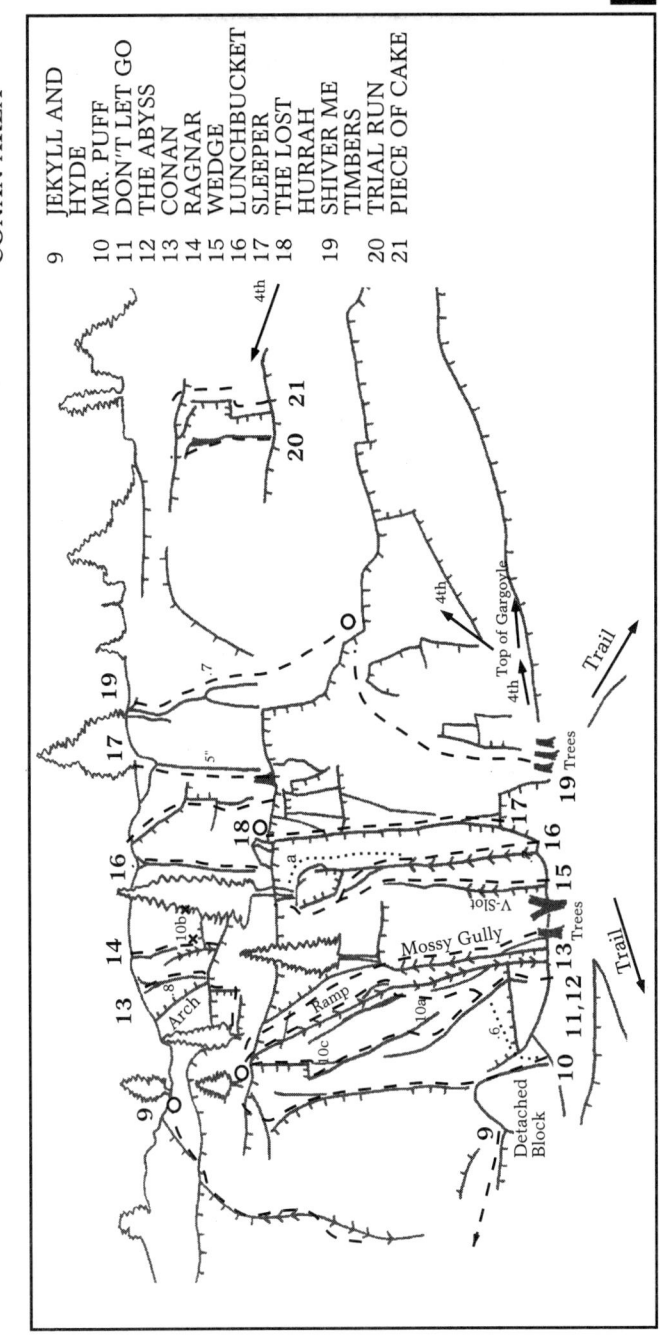

EASTERN SHORE

rightmost crack, which leads up the increasingly steep face to the left side of a small roof. Step right and climb the crack up the right side of the roof. Scramble off left or join Conan.

Pro: Somewhat difficult to place at times, but good. SLCDs useful. A long pitch, for the Paces Lake area.

12**   THE ABYSS   5.9
FA: Sean Willett
May 1992

Climbs a thin crack and arete on the right side of the red, mottled face. At the top of the thin crack, swing to the right, around the corner and onto a low-angle ramp, follow the left edge, which leads to the ledge at the top of the face.

Pro: Wired chocks for the thin crack, medium to large SLCDs for the flaring cracks on the upper ramp.

13   CONAN   P.1   5.6
                    P.2***   **5.8**
FA: Tony Veling and Dan Price
June 1982

The first pitch, starting in a mossy gully, is usually wet and dirty, and is not recommended. The second pitch climbs a short dihedral to a ledge at the base of a left-leaning, fist-sized jamcrack. Follow this crack on awkward jams up to and over the small bulge at the top, to finish by a large erratic boulder on top. The second pitch is enjoyable and provides a nice finish to the climbs on the red, mottled face to the left of the first pitch. The first pitch provides a winter ice climb, on occasion.

Pro: Medium SLCDs useful for the upper jamcrack.

14*   **RAGNAR**   **5.10b**
            FA: Sean Willett and Dan Price
            August 8, 1991

Start from the ledge at the base of the final jamcrack on Conan. Climb directly up the arete or the face to the right, past a bolt (5.10b), into a jamcrack (5.6), and onto the top of the buttress.
Pro: One bolt, small to medium chocks or SLCDs for the upper crack.

15*   **WEDGE**   **5.7**
            FA: Tony Veling and Kevin Cody
            June 1987

A preferred alternative to the first pitches of Conan or Lunchbucket (see description 16). Start in the shallow, right-facing dihedral between Conan and Lunchbucket. The start can be identified by a large, forked birch tree one metre to the left. Climb the acute, wedge-shaped dihedral and the cracks above to join Lunchbucket just below the belay ledge.
Pro: Well-protected by a standard rack.

16   **LUNCHBUCKET** **P.1** **5.7**
                             P.2 **5.7**
            FA: Tony Veling and Dan Price
            June 1982

This dirty, mossy, often wet groove is badly in need of cleaning. Climb the dirty groove until it forks at an overhanging block. Swing left around the overhang to a ramp with a large tree. Climb the ramp and a steep crack to the belay ledge. The second pitch follows a second dirty, vegetated groove above to the top.
Pro: Standard rack.

16a   VARIATION   5.7
          FA: Kevin Cody and Mike Moyles

A more-interesting alternative. At the overhanging block, move right and follow a steep corner and crack back left to rejoin the original route just below the belay ledge.

Pro: Standard rack.

17   SLEEPER P.1   5.7
                  P.2 ***   5.6
          FA: Tony Veling and Dan Price
          June 1982

This enjoyable and well-protected climb starts from the ledge two metres above, and immediately to the right of, the start of the Lunchbucket groove. Climb the obvious cracks and dihedrals over a series of ledges, trending left to a belay ledge that has a large block perched on its edge. Several variations are possible on the first pitch; the second pitch climbs the chimney and fist-sized crack behind the large tree to the top.

Pro: Well-protected by a standard rack.

18*   THE LOST HURRAH   5.7
           FA: Kevin Cody and Tony Veling
           June 1987

Start just left of the second pitch on Sleeper. Climb an overhanging face into a left-slanting ramp, which leads to the upper slab.

Pro: Good with standard rack.

19**   **SHIVER ME TIMBERS**   **5.7**

FA: Mike Moyles and Kevin Cody

Climb the first pitch of Sleeper or scramble up from the right. The second pitch climbs an excellent jamcrack, which curves left up the steep face. The rotten tree that protruded from the middle of the crack—giving the climb its name—has since departed this world; only the stump remains.

Pro: Medium SLCDs useful for the second pitch.

20   **TRIAL RUN**   **5.8**

FA: Ted Johnston and Tony Veling

This ten-metre climb follows a flaring slot and crack just left of the big roof of Piece of Cake (see description 21).

Pro: Standard rack.

21*   **PIECE OF CAKE**   **5.8**

FA: Kevin Cody and Tony Veling
June 1987

Scramble up a series of ledges and steps from the base of Sleeper to a ledge at the elevation of the first belay of Sleeper and Shiver Me Timbers. Can also be reached by scrambling up from the right starting near Buffy (see "The Deep South End," description 6). Start in a corner under a big roof a mere three metres above the ledge. Climb out from under the roof and lieback up the crack above. Short and fun.

Pro: Good. Medium to large SLCDs useful.

THE DEEP SOUTH END

These are a collection of climbs on a spur of the South Buttress that extends down to the lakeshore.

ROUTE DESCRIPTIONS

1*   **VORTICITY**   **5.10a**
FA: Sean Willett, Pat Wheatley, and Peter Gilliver
September 13, 1992

This route climbs the steep corner to the left of the Gargoyle wall (see description 2). The going is awkward at first, with an interesting exit from the steep wall to join On the Brink.
Pro: Difficult to place at the bottom, then good. Small to medium SLCDs useful.

2***   **GARGOYLE**   **5.12a**
FA: Sean Willett
August 1992   *Sport Climb*

Two overhanging walls meet in a distinctive prow near the lakeshore; Gargoyle, a wildly overhanging climb, extends across the left wall to finish directly on the prow. Start at the far left of the wall, traversing right on the undercling flake. Head up to the horizontal ledge, then right to finish directly over the nose of the prow. Nick Sagar made a notable early repeat of this climb.
Pro: Three bolts and chains. Two warnings: Climbers who top-rope without clipping the bolts are commonly impaled on the tree by the water; and the bolt to the lower right is a project that leads nowhere.

DEEP SOUTH END

83

1. VORTICITY
2. GARGOYLE
3. ON THE BRINK
4. LICHEN VIRGIN
5. DIRTY, WET AND LOOSE
6. BUFFY
7. FAREWELL TO ARMS

EASTERN SHORE

3**   ON THE BRINK   5.7
FA: Sean Willett
and Heather Reynolds
August 1992

Follow the exposed upper lip of the overhanging wall marking the edge of the Lichen Virgin slab (see description 4). Start on the mossy ledges in the trees, climbing up and left. Traverse left just below the chains on Gargoyle, then follow cracks on the arete to the ledge on top. Rappel from the tree or scramble off to the left.

Pro: Well-protected with a standard rack.

4*   LICHEN VIRGIN   5.7
FA: Heather Reynolds
and Alan Gilchrist
July 1992

Start on mossy ledges in the trees to the right of the overhanging wall. Climb slightly left to gain a crack that leads up to an overhanging flaring slot, then continue up the slot to a large ledge with a tree. To avoid the slot, move left, climbing directly up the prow to the ledge. Rappel from the tree or scramble off to the left.

Pro: Well-protected with a standard rack.

5   DIRTY, WET AND LOOSE   5.6
FA: Heather Reynolds
and Andrea Losier
September 13, 1992

Follow the left-angling break at the top of the Lichen Virgin slab, starting at the base of the steep gully. There is some loose rock.

Pro: Standard rack.

6   BUFFY   5.9
   FA: Sean Willett, Adam Hartling, and Brian Merry
   July 25, 1992

Climb a short, steep dihedral about twenty-five metres up the slope from Gargoyle, watching out for some loose rock.

Pro: Only fair, but not bad. RPs and small wires useful.

7   FAREWELL
       TO ARMS   5.9**
   FA: Kevin Cody and Phil Fisher

This climb is on a separate crag at the far right side of the area, near the water. The route includes a very nice fifteen-metre left-trending finger-and-hand crack.

Pro: Very good with standard rack and some medium SLCDs.

NEVERLAND

Neverland is a small crag on Paces Lake south of the Main Face, well-hidden in a small side gully. Although the crag is a mere hundred metres from the shore, only the top slab can be seen from the lake; and Neverland remained unknown until Peter Gilliver, Sean Willett, and Keir Willett came upon it during extensive search of the hills around Paces Lake in 1993. A real find, Neverland is a beautiful fifteen-metre crag that boasts the hardest climb to date in Nova Scotia. Overhanging on all its major faces (the main wall overhangs more than six metres over its sixteen metres), Neverland's several climbs are excellent and steep.

There is also a series of ice climbs just south of the Neverland rock-climbing area, the most accessible of which forms just south of the small cove south of the trail into Neverland. The climb, just above the lake, is about fifteen metres long. Several variations are possible, and all are about grade III (moderate) in difficulty. Farther south, around the next point and back in the woods, await a series of other climbs. Depending on ice conditions, several five- to eight-metre free-standing pillars may be found. These climbs are not visible from the lake (except the one farthest south), and are all considerable harder than the climbs by the cove at Neverland (grade III to V).

APPROACH
Neverland can be reached overland by following the lakeshore south from the Main Face.

About five hundred metres south, a small stream joins the lake in a sheltered cove; a large boulder overhanging the lake serves as a landmark. The crag is one hundred metres up the stream bed; the trail from the lake is flagged. When approaching by boat, watch for the overhanging boulder and the small cove; land just north of the boulder.

Peter Gilliver searches for holds on Lost Boys, in the Neverland area.

ROUTE DESCRIPTIONS

1**   NO GROWNUPS   5.11a
FA: Sean Willett
September 1993   *Sport Climb*
Follow flakes in the corner, then out right onto the overhanging wall. A last hard move gains the ledge.
Pro: Four bolts and chains.

2***   HAPPY THOUGHTS 5.11d/12a
FA: Sean Willett
September 1993
A beautiful, sharp-edged fist crack leads up to a rest stance under a small roof. A thin crack, which splits the entire crag, exits the roof to the right and leads through the overhanging headwall. The crack thins towards the top, leaving the climber to make some desperate face moves to the right and the top. This crack splits the entire crag and is very obvious on top.
Pro: Wires to large SLCDs. Top is run-out, but safe.

2a**   VARIATION   5.9
At the roof at the top of the fist crack, traverse left to the chains on No Grownups.

3***   THE LOST BOYS   5.12c
FA: Sean Willett
September 25, 1993   *Sport Climb*
Currently the hardest ascent in the region, this wild sport climb follows a series of small flakes directly up the centre of the overhanging main wall. A good rest at the halfway

point keeps this climb from receiving an even harder grade. Top-roping requires clipping bolts to prevent a huge swing off into the trees.

Pro: Seven bolts, mostly glue-in rings; lower-off rings.

3a** VARIATION   5.12c
       FA: Project   *Sport Climb*

A two-bolt variation to the left of the standard start. About the same difficulty.

Pro: Seven bolts in all.

4   **THE FAIRY CRACK 5.11a**
        FA: Sean Willett
        April 1993

This climb, which follows the excellent, sharp-edged crack on the right side of the main wall, starts out offhand size, but quickly gets wider and easier. Rappel off from the ledge at the top of the crack.

Pro: SLCDs very, very useful.

5*   **PROJECT**   **5.10**
       FA: Project

This route climbs an overhanging dihedral on the west face of the crag. It should be leadable on natural gear.

EASTERN SHORE

GIBRALTAR ROCK

Continuing northwest on Highway 357 about eight kilometres past the Paces Lake turn-off is a small crag on the right (north) side of the road. It is most significant for its ice-climbing in winter; although conditions fluctuate dramatically, the gullies and slabs can sport a considerable amount of ice. There is also some rock potential.

GIBRALTAR LAKE

A canoe is required for the approach: cross the Musquodoboit and paddle up a small side estuary to reach a fire road. Portage about three hundred metres up this road to reach Gibraltar Lake. There is a small crag on the northwest corner of the lake, still awaiting first ascents.

HOWE LAKE

There is a small, undeveloped crag easily accessed by a logging road that turns off Highway 357 a few miles west of the Paces Lake exit. The road is gated, but a brief hike leads to the cliff, just short of Howe Lake. No routes have been developed, but many easy-to-moderate climbs await the enthusiastic explorer well-equipped with cleaning hardware.

SALMON RIVER LAKE

Several fine, undeveloped cliffs await on Salmon River Lake, just east of the Musquodoboit Valley. The approach is long and requires a boat. Either paddle up the eastern arm of Jeddore Harbour and portage up the Salmon River, or approach from Eel Pond near Musquodoboit Harbour and portage over to Salmon Lake. There is a small crag on the southeast corner of the lake, and there are two large domes just north of the lake; these last require a fair bushwhack to reach.

SHIP ROCK

Ship Rock is the best of the undeveloped cliffs included in this guide. Although somewhat difficult to approach, being on an island, it has the potential for a dozen or so routes. Ship Rock, like Eagles Rock, is quartzite of the Goldenville Formation, but in contrast to Eagles Rock it has many good crack climbs.

Ship Rock, a largely unclimbed crag on the Eastern Shore.

APPROACH

Ship Rock is an island less than a kilometre off shore, just east of Ship Harbour, an hour east of Halifax. Leave Route 7 just west of Murphy Cove, heading towards the Murphy Cove campground and dock. Park at the campground—but ask the proprietors first, as the lot gets crowded during the season. This is a popular area for sea kayaking, and a map of the islands is available in the campground office. The climbing on Ship Rock is on the southwest side, so it is best to head down "the Tickles," a narrow passage, and approach the island from the west. There is a sheltered cove northwest of the cliff with a trail leading from there to the top.

NATURE OF THE CLIMBING

No routes have been developed at Ship Rock, although some climbs have been top-roped. With a height of nearly twenty metres, there is good potential. A series of cracks on the left side, starting just above a huge roof, are in the 5.9 to hard 5.10 range. The roof cutting across the middle of the cliff *might* be climbable, but it certainly *can* be climbed to the right, where several potential routes lead directly up the centre of the cliff. Farther to the right, there is potential for more climbing, but the rock is very dirty, being a popular eating spot for local waterfowl (to put it bluntly, the rock is covered in seagull guano). Many climbs are leadable on natural gear, but, like the quartzite at Eagles Rock, the cracks tend to be angular and flared, and do not easily take some chocks. Small SLCDs will probably work best.

Nova Scotia's scenic South Shore is comprised primarily of granite, and one would expect to find good climbing opportunities throughout the region. However, if good climbing exits, it has not yet been discovered—developed, documented climbing is limited to a few small sea cliffs and bouldering locales. More climbing is undoubtedly possible and will one day be brought to the attention of climbers.

CHEBUCTO HEAD

The South Shore of Nova Scotia is famous for its scenic lighthouses, one of which sits atop Chebucto Head. The rocky granite headland provides not only a prime location for a lighthouse, but also a climbing opportunity. The cliffs directly below the lighthouse are neither extensive nor high, but the rock is excellent and clean, and provides excellent bouldering. There is a gully cutting in towards the lighthouse with side walls large enough to warrant a top-rope, or even a short lead. To get there, follow Highway 379 south of Halifax and watch for the turnoff to Chebucto Head. Park by the lighthouse and hike directly down towards the water.

TERENCE BAY

Several bands of steep granite are visible across the water, from the government wharf in the town of Terence Bay. Some crags rise directly out of the bay, but the largest cliff is set back from the water by about twenty metres. This cliff is about eighteen metres high and overhangs for its entire extent. A series of cracks provide climbable weaknesses, but the overhanging nature of the cliff makes even the easiest of these lines difficult; consequently, only one of the major lines has been climbed. The others await bolder visitors.

APPROACH

The best way to approach is by boat from Terence Bay, a twenty-minute drive south of Halifax. The bay is not very well protected, so be careful of rough seas. With calm seas, it is possible to land on the rocks below the main cliff; otherwise, there is a sheltered cove to the left of the crag. Hikers have been encountered at the cliff, so it must also be possible to reach it by foot.

ROUTE DESCRIPTIONS

1   WATER SLIDE   5.6
             FA: Alan Gilchrist and Sean Willett
             May 22, 1992

This short route follows the low-angle slab and thin crack just above the water.
Pro: Wires and small SLCDs useful.

2*   LAND AND SEA   5.10d
             FA: Sean Willett
             May 22, 1992

Follow one of the main overhanging crack lines in the centre of the wall, taking a direct line for the full eighteen metres of climbing and finishing by a small tree just below and to the right of the top. The climb includes cracks from finger to offwidth size.
Pro: Sometimes strenuous to place. Small to medium SLCDs useful.

PEGGYS COVE

The picturesque fishing village and lighthouse at Peggys Cove is one of Nova Scotia's most famous tourist destinations. The scenic attraction owes much to a long granite headland, swept clean by exposure to the open Atlantic storms. Although the coast does not have much relief for climbing, the clean white granite provides excellent bouldering.

Bouldering above the waves at Peggys Cove. Photo: Sylvia Fuller

Peggys Cove is easy to find: just follow the signs on Highway 333 from Halifax. Park in the enormous lot by the restaurant near the lighthouse. There is some bouldering near the lighthouse, but the best is found a few hundred metres northeast along the shore. It is possible to walk along the rocky ledges for hours, finding small climbing gems along the way. A rope can allow some climbing above the water. The surf is extremely dangerous, so be careful near the water.

There is also climbing along the highway in the direction of Halifax. For example, look for a small lake or swamp a few kilometres east of Peggys Cove, on the ocean side of the road. A trail follows the east side of the water and passes several good-sized boulders on the way to a small beach, which also has some decent bouldering.

PADDYS HEAD

Not far from Peggys Cove, along the St. Margaret's Bay shore, stands a small crag overlooking the water. Just north of the town of Indian Harbour, five kilometres from Peggys Cove on Highway 333, a paved road turns off and runs along the coast to a point called Paddys Head. By parking a few hundred metres short of a bridge leading out to the head and hiking towards the ocean, you may be able to find this small, well-hidden climbing spot. The ten-metre cliff rises directly out of the water, so top-roping is the standard technique. Climbs are mostly moderate (under 5.7).

LIVERPOOL

Farther down the South Shore, climbing opportunities are scarce or have not yet been discovered. Not to be completely deprived, climbers near Liverpool, ninety minutes south of Halifax, have been using a large roadcut on Exit 19 off Highway 103. Like most roadcuts, this one suffers from large quantities of dirty, loose rock; but there are some clean slabs, and the maximum height of fifteen metres is significant. This crag may not become a destination, but if you find yourself on the South Shore, it is worth doing—not least because of the nice view of the Mersey River Valley from the top of the crags, and the not insignificant amenity of a Tim Hortons a mere two minutes down the road towards Liverpool.

Roadcuts on both sides of the highway have been climbed: the west side, beside the southbound exit ramp, is larger. Top-roping trees are available, but set back quite far from the cliff, so a long sling is needed.

ROUTE DESCRIPTIONS
WEST SIDE

1   TICK SLAB   5.4-5.6
Climb the long, low-angle slab at the far left end.

2   TIM HORTONS   5.5-5.7
Follow an inside corner with two small overhangs.

3   WRONG WAY   5.7
Start behind the Wrong Way sign. This is the cleanest route to date.

EAST SIDE

1   FISH SCALES   5.6

This route, about halfway along the outcrop, follows a series of small edges.